Friendships
The Aspie Way

Wendy Lawson

Foreword by Emma Wall

Jessica Kingsley Publishers
London and Philadelphia

First published in 2006
by Jessica Kingsley Publishers
116 Pentonville Road
London N1 9JB, UK
and
400 Market Street, Suite 400
Philadelphia, PA 19106, USA

www.jkp.com

Copyright © Wendy Lawson 2006
Foreword copyright © Emma Wall 2006

Illustrations by Megan Quinn

Library of Congress Cataloging in Publication Data
A CIP catalog record for this book is available from the Library of Congress

British Library Cataloguing in Publication Data
A CIP catalogue record for this book is available from the British Library

ISBN-13: 978 1 84310 427 8
ISBN-10: 1 84310 427 X

Printed and bound in Great Britain by
Athenaeum Press, Gateshead, Tyne and Wear

For Gillian, my friend
from Ivy Lane Junior School,
Chippenham, Wiltshire,
England, in 1962.
When no one else listened,
you sat me upon your bicycle,
pushed that bicycle for three miles
and took me home.
We were nine years old.
I was too ill to walk.

You saved my life...

Contents

Acknowledgements

Several months ago, when I began to write this book, I had no idea of the impact it would have upon me. I liked the idea of a book on friendship, but I didn't realise it would mean my own friendships and relational experiences might be highlighted. I guess I was naive in this respect. Because of the subject material for this book, 'Friendship' has occupied my thinking in a dramatic way; I've needed to examine its nooks and crannies. I've also had to look at my own friendship skills and revisit the reasons for my friendships. It's been a bit tough at times. I'm an Aspie! My literal-ness means that I can take my friends literally: 'Call me any time, Wendy.' I have. It can also mean that I open my life to abuse. With regard to the above, I have experienced the extremes of both. I want to thank Jessica Kingsley (my friend) for encouraging me to write this book.

I want to say a big thank you to all my friends who have personally contributed to this book by adding their own words. I also want to thank all those friends who haven't written within the pages of this book but who have most definitely written into my life experiences in one way or another (Gracie, Mr Chris, Michael and Elizabeth; Mick, Rose and Thomo; Alice, Pierre and Jessie; Mr John; Debs and Josie; Mr Mouse; Cousin Julie; Carolyn Brown and Adrian; Suzette Young; Karen Stagnitti; Helen and Bob; Helen, Peter and Ben; Jan; Amanda Golding; all the guys from 'High Fliers', Janine, Wendy, Peter and Davin (to name a few). Word limits on this book prohibit my including all of my friends literally, but you are all here!

I usually think of myself as someone with just a few friends. What I have come to realise is that I actually have more friends than I had thought.

To you all, THANK YOU! I wish you true and dear friendship in all your life adventures.

Foreword

In one of Wendy's previous books (*Life Behind Glass*, 1998) she writes, 'Why is it that someone can say they want to get to know you, share their lives with you, and then pull away when you disappoint them or become too demanding?' In the intervening years and in the process of writing this book it seems to me that Wendy has sought an answer to this and many other friendship questions.

Wendy is the perfect person to have written this book; she is an expert in the field of Asperger's syndrome – living with it and excelling in a mostly neurotypical world. She is also a wonderful friend.

I met Wendy at university in 1993. Wendy was and still is a dedicated, focused and hard-working student. I was, and still am, focused on many different things at once – only one of them being university. Despite these differences, we forged a long-lasting friendship.

Wendy is a constant source of inspiration. Wendy's Asperger's is not a disability, it is a difference. Part of friendship is in knowing what your friends like, how to make your home a comfortable place for them to visit – whether to cook chicken or tofu – whether to offer beer or mineral water – or play hard rock or folk music, and so on. Wendy is no more different than any other of my friends. She is as unique as any of them. That's what makes life interesting.

There are things of great beauty that Wendy will stop and notice whilst the rest of us simply pass by. At other times Wendy will pass by the superficial (upon which others may be fixated) and continue to focus on the task at hand.

Whatever factors have come to impact Wendy's life, she has chosen to look them square in the face. She takes each challenge that life brings her way and responds to each situation so as to create a strong sense of self; a powerful sense of purpose and a positive impact on those of us who are lucky enough to call ourselves 'her friend'.

As a friend, an educator and as a person with Asperger's, Wendy has, I believe, amazing communicative qualities. She is direct, honest, inspiring and open. These qualities are reflected in this book as Wendy brings you on a journey of exploration of the complexities of friendship – through the stumbling blocks and the realisations.

I consider myself extremely lucky to have learnt from Wendy's insight and knowledge over the years – I'm sure that once you've read this book you will begin to understand why.

Wendy's laugh warms my heart, her intelligence stimulates my mind and her determination is a constant reminder that life is there to be lived to the fullest.

Thanks, Wendy.

Emma Wall

Emma Wall is a Melbourne-based independent singer songwriter. She spends much of the year on the road – bringing her urban funky folk music to venues and festivals throughout Australia and North America. Emma has studied psychology, theology and philosophy, as well as business management and communication skills. Most of the time she prefers singing songs. To find out more you can visit www.emmawall.com.

Introduction

Although I certainly understand the concept of 'friend' now, as a child I didn't understand this. The concept that other people were separate from me was not a consideration. If I thought a thought, I believed others would know what I was thinking. Therefore, they must have known what I needed. Failure to meet my needs resulted in my feeling angry, hurt and unimportant. Even now, as an adult, I still 'feel' that the other person might know what is happening for me because *I feel it*. Academically, however, I know that only I know what is going on in my head and heart. But, because the feeling is so strong for me, I still need frequently to check out that the other person doesn't 'feel' it too! Imagine the effect on your friendships if you believed your friends knew stuff about you but did nothing about it.

Tony Attwood (1998) tells us a story about a young girl with Asperger's syndrome who, uninvited, began to tell an approaching postman all about Deltic locomotives. Even when she asked the postman a question (about the trains of course), she didn't understand that she needed to wait for him to answer. She continued on with her one-sided conversation until the postman blurted out a hurried 'goodbye' and left. Could things have gone differently if this young girl had understood the rules about conversational interaction? Was she attempting to be friendly, but hadn't understood how? Why do so many of us, as individuals on the autism spectrum, find it difficult to be 'in tune' with others?

When I was asked to write this book I felt a sense of surprise and amazement. 'Me, write a book on friendship!' I exclaimed. 'I'm not so good at "friends" and quite a number of "friends" I once had are not on my current friendship list.' 'Well that's their loss,' my colleague said. 'I think you do friendship rather well.' Wow, this was a new concept to me. I had never thought of myself as 'doing well at friendship stuff'. In fact, for me, I'd thought the opposite to be true. I seem to have the knack of upsetting people. Many of the individuals I had counted as my friends were no longer my friends. Most of those people, if I met them, might still be polite and even friendly towards me, but they would not see themselves as 'Wendy's friends'. Most of the time they remain aloof, distant and in my past, not present, life. Usually some action I had taken was the reason for their distance. For example, they didn't agree with my choice of partner or career, the house I lived in or my belief systems.

Autism and Asperger's

Being a person with an autism spectrum diff-ability (ASD) means I'm designed to use a monotropic attention system that influences my thoughts, words and deeds (Murray, Lesser and Lawson 2005). Monotropic attention implies 'having few interests highly aroused' which leads to 'tending to perform the task well and tending to lose awareness of information relevant to other tasks' (pp.140–141). So, if I naturally focus from and to any one matter at any one time (within my interest system), but find it difficult to focus outside of that interest system, sharing in conversation and activity, with friends, might not be easy.

For all of us, on the autism spectrum or not, one's attentive attributes are part of one's cognitive state. It is our cognitive design that enables processing of information and prepares us for action (whether in thought, word or deed). Typical individuals tend towards dividing their attention. This will lead them into having many interests less highly aroused (Murray *et al.* 2005). If one's cognitive and subsequent actions are guided by mono-tropism (the main river for focused energy, attention, etc.) and its many tributaries (for example, being literal, thinking in closed concepts, having difficulties with forward thinking, etc.), it will mean using energy and attention in only one direction and one domain at any one time. This has implications for many areas in one's life: sensory, emotional, physical, environmental, educational, and so on.

In practical terms, for many of us less typical individuals, outside of our specific areas of interest, we are not good at dividing our attention and energy to accommodate the usual many bits of information that are coming in our direction, all at once. Many of my friends, however, are good with dividing their attention and energies, so they can accommodate their own interests and the interests of others, no problem. Physically and mentally, therefore, because we each operate on different planes of attention, we can miss one another. Misconception, misconstrued concepts and misgivings are commonplace amongst us.

Therefore, many of us, as less typical individuals, try so hard to accommodate a world that is multi-channelled and insists on multi-tasking, so we use up huge amounts of energy trying to comply with the demand upon us and we are often exhausted by the effort. This has consequences for friendship. In typical individuals, dividing attention comes naturally. Therefore, typical individuals can process information and be actively engaged in a number of events simultaneously. It's often not a problem for them to think and feel at the same time. In friendships, they employ these activities on a regular basis. They chat, walk, process, eat and modify their behaviour all at once! They are even able to put their own interests on hold to accommodate the interests of others. Unfortunately, for many of us, less typical individuals, one is expected to do and to be the same as typical individuals. But, for many of us it's difficult to talk and think, difficult to talk and do, etc. We tend not to function well in multi-tasking situations, unless they are primed by our interest systems which are harnessed by our attention.

So, when my own interest system is aroused, I can focus and attend to something for hours without apparently feeling tired. When my friends join my attention tunnel, we can be happily engaged for ages! On other occasions though, in the company of friends who are chatting about things that are difficult for me to attend to, my interest can wander. For example, at times when I have been out walking with a friend, I spot a bird (one of my passions is bird watching); though my attention will be diverted, and it could occur during any conversation, my friends might not appreciate this; they might feel rejected and interrupted, especially when it happens frequently! They assume that I am not interested in them or that I don't want to talk to them. This isn't the case at all. What is happening, however, is that I only have single attention available to me and this can be wholly occupied by my interests, so much so that it means other interests cannot be accommodated. I don't want to have my interest taken away, this is not the answer, but I might need to learn how to widen the window of attention so that I can tap into interests outside of my own.

With the above in mind, it's easy to understand how we, as less typical individuals on the autism and Aspie spectrum, tend to find the whole arena of friendship rather complicated. Having said this, I'm told that even typical individuals can find friendship difficult. It seems that making and maintaining friendships is a bit of an art.

Some literature I have read concerning autism and Asperger's states that individuals on the ASD spectrum tend towards not wanting friends and/or not doing well at friendship. I dispute this argument and suggest, instead, that many of us do want friends but are unsure of the process involved. I hope that this book will unravel the friendship mystery for many and, therefore, make friendship more available and less daunting.

Belief systems

I'm fortunate, I have some beautiful friends who have stuck with me through all weathers and, even when they don't agree with me over something, this has not negatively influenced their availability to me as my friends. My friends have learnt to understand Wendy's idiosyncrasies!

Sometimes we can 'lose' friends (they leave our friendship) out of no fault of our own. Sometimes we lose friends because of some stupid or silly thing we did. Then, there are those occasions we lose friends because of negative belief systems that have predisposed us to low self-esteem and a lack of confidence. This can translate to our believing that we are unworthy of friends or that friends will eventually leave us when they discover what we are really like. Let me explain.

As human beings we each grow up in families that may have either a positive or negative impact upon us as developing adults. As adults we each contribute to the belief systems of our particular family, by perpetuating and nurturing those beliefs. According to Young and Klosko (1993), the things we believe about ourselves and about others can become 'lifetraps', particularly if they keep us prisoners to negative and destructive outcomes. What if such lifetraps were behind the various relational problems that plague so many of us?

Some psychological theories, such as cognitive theory, suggest that as well as being the product of genes (nature) we each contribute to who we are by what we think. Therefore, if we change our negative thinking to that of a more positive image, our emotive responses to our circumstances may change for the better. Cognitive theory suggests the art of being a positive person with good self-esteem and confidence is based in our having positive cognitive perceptions of ourselves and of how others view us. When we experience ourselves positively, the argument is that we exude confidence, which makes our company more desirable to others; therefore, we are more likely to attract 'friends'. Maybe this is where the proverb 'to have friends one needs to be friendly' comes from.

Schema theory, on the other hand, suggests that our belief systems and potential outcomes from those beliefs are deeply rooted and enmeshed within one's personality, upbringing, interaction with family and peers and personal decisions. It proposes that these are evident in what one experiences in one's valued outcomes. The idea of schemata, a Piagetian (1963) term used to illustrate how one might access the 'scheme' of things and lay down the foundation for core belief systems within the brain, suggests that such core belief systems are routes or tracks that become established over time and are not easily remedied or challenged. In fact, it is usual for one to maintain the status quo in order for one's body and mind to feel 'right'. For example, an individual controlled by an abandonment schema might believe the following: 'I know ultimately my friends will reject me; so I will keep them at a safe distance and not allow them to get too close to me.' Although this thinking might be at a subconscious level, it is acted out in daily relationships. The action from the abandonment schema will send a message to the friends of the individual concerned, and they will perceive that they are not valued as friends and may eventually exit the friendship. Their responses confirm the thinking of the individual – 'Yep, you see, I knew you would leave me' – and this keeps the confirmation going that they will always, ultimately, be abandoned by everyone.

Understanding concepts that have contributed to the beliefs of ourselves (cognitive or schematic), taking the time to challenge them and ultimately learning how to take back the control over our lives, could assist us with creating more positive friendships. So, why be controlled by the past and the schemata that once occupied our cognitive and emotive development, if we don't have to?

Being able to visualise the cognitive and schematic processes involved with the development of understanding ourselves and then choosing to rewrite them in a form that is more positive will open doors for a happier and healthier future. When one considers that most neurologically typically developing individuals (typical people) function best in the social arena with the developing knowledge that self is a reflection of societal norms, customs, traditions and accepted practices, then it is no wonder that confusion and miscommunication reign in so many of our relationships. The difficulty for some of us is that we may not have come from a place of positive interaction and acceptance. Many of the societies we live in are not inclusive of difference. Hence, in its most rigid form, society perpetuates modes of behaviour that prevent the healthy development of positive self-esteem and ability in a varied and wide population of individuals. For many of us, therefore, we have not had a good template to base the concepts of friendship upon. In developing my own template, I've lost a few friends and found some others. I've made some mistakes and I've won some battles. In all of my developing relationships I've learnt stuff!

Even though this is so, I still feel a sense of sadness when I remember friends that are no longer in my life. However, even though there is no guarantee that any friendship we invest in will stand the test of time, making and having friends is a very good thing. Even if we have a friend for a season and not a lifetime, that season is probably better than a season without that friendship.

Some of our friendships are formed because we share a common goal. This could mean that when the goal is achieved we move on; having nothing else in common, those friendships can wane. Other friendships are based on more solid ground, and their foundations are built out of mutual love and care that is determined to ride the storms of life with us, no matter what. So, even when we fail, disappoint, disagree with and even desert a friend, our friends stay true to us!

'I always spell that word [friend] wrong,' I said to Emma. 'It's so hard to remember which comes first, the *i* or the *e*.' 'I have a good way to remember which one comes first,' Emma said. 'The word "friend" means that the person will be there for you, no matter what. So, the last three letters at the end of the word spell "end", because there is no end to their friendship.' I certainly found Emma's words very helpful and I value her friendship. However, not all of the individuals I had thought of as my friends have lived up to the term!

So, this book is a book about friendship. It explores the concept of friendship, what it might mean and how one might go about the business of building and maintaining friendships. For any good relationship to be ongoing it will need fuel, as a fire does, or it will simply fizzle out. What kinds of fuel do friendships need? What happens when times are tough and friends are scarce? Can we learn to be our own best friend? Does being a 'good friend' to someone else come naturally or does it take a bit of work? Read on to discover the answers to these, and many other, questions.

Not all of our friends are human. Some would say, 'Man's (or woman's) best friend is his (or her) dog.' Think about the role our pets play as our friends. There certainly is evidence that stroking your cat can lower blood pressure and steady a crumbling heart!

As well as exploring friendship building and maintenance, this book also explores what might be happening within our personal belief systems that could sabotage our friendships. These ideas, along with practical examples, poetry and illustrative stories, can be discovered within the following pages.

References

Attwood, T. (1998) *Asperger's Syndrome: A Guide for Parents and Professionals.* London: Jessica Kingsley Publishers.

Murray, D.K.C., Lesser, M. and Lawson, W. (2005) 'Attention, monotropism and the diagnostic criteria for autism.' *International Journal of Research and Practice: Autism 9*, 2, 139–156.

Piaget, J. (1963) *The Psychology of Intelligence.* New York: Routledge.

Young, J. and Klosko, J. (1993) *Reinventing Your Life.* New York: Plume Books.

CHAPTER 1

What Is a Friend?

The term 'friend' probably means differ-ent things to different people. However, essentially it means someone who is on your side and who will want to be a good companion to you and have you be a good companion to them. Learning to be our own best friend is something I am becoming aware of and, perhaps, is a concept not explored nearly enough. Just like the problems with self-acceptance and building a sure foundation for friendship. These are discussed more in Chapter 6.

What kinds of friends are there? We can have human, animal and material companions. I say 'material' not to represent some kind of beloved fabric so much as beloved material goods. At times, an object of affection, like a car, a jewel, a toy or some other object, can be the centre of our world.

Some individuals even have 'imaginary' friends. This is not uncommon for children, especially if they are an 'only' child. At times some of our human friends, who may be companions, are also members of our families: our sisters, brothers, mothers, fathers, uncles, aunts, cousins and grandparents.

Sometimes we can have a companion who is a pet: our bird, dog, cat, budgie, goldfish, reptile, guinea pig, rabbit or hamster, and so on. Then, of course, there are those individuals who are not related to us by blood or family ties, but cross our path as we each journey through life. We may meet at school, college, work, church or some other place. Some of us find our best friends via the Internet. In fact, for some of us, relating to another person 'on-line' can be really rewarding.

 The computer, as a medium for communication, seems to work very well for me. I can take my time to compose my words, check what I am writing and change it if I want to. I find that there is less interference when I'm relating via the computer too. For example, the things that can cause my thoughts to be interrupted (the movements on someone's face or body) are not there. This means I can think and process information more clearly. It's very important to access clear communication with one's friends, so having the time to process information that is passing between us is vital.

In a friendship magazine on-line I once read that to be a 'proper' friend one must make time for friends. The article went on to say that email, rather than being a blessing, was actually a hindrance to developing and maintaining friendships. Email was lumped in the same category as speaking on a mobile phone. It was suggested that email and mobile phone messages were more an exchange of information that was tagged on to other activities; kind of like 'half-baked' and not the full thing.

> That's because one or both parties are doing something else while conversing: trawling the aisles of a supermarket, maybe, or driving the motorways. And when the person you're conversing with isn't able to give you her full attention, it's hard, if not impossible, to feel heard, let alone understood. It fails to comfort because it's not nurturing – kind of the way popcorn fails to satisfy, even if you eat a bucketful, because it's not nourishing. (*Ladies' Home Journal* on-line: www.lhj.com)

This might be the case for typical individuals who tend to need to do several things at once, but, for many of us less typical individuals, this may not be so.

As individuals with ASD we tend to be less typical than some other people. We tend to put all of our attention and energy into these mediums because that's the way we are made. Dividing our attention between several different things goes against the grain. In fact, it is because of our need to use single attention that we can use email as a very good medium via which to communicate and to nurture our friendships. I'm not so sure about mobile phones, but then again I have run up enormous phone bills (mobile) because of long conversations to a dear friend over my phone (but not whilst driving a car!).

So I guess I'm saying that to be a friend there are all sorts of ways and means that facilitate friendliness and show our willingness to listen to others. But for many of us Aspies and Auties, the conventional methods might be difficult – going shopping together, doing lunch, meeting with the lads down the pub, being part of a club or church, and so on. Not that these activities are out of reach for us or can't be done, just that they take lots of attention and quickly wear us out. So, they might need to be kept to a minimum, and for us, email, due to the reasoning outlined above, may play a larger role in finding and maintaining friendships than it does for typical individuals.

Friendship

I like the way I feel when my friends are real.
Real friends.
I like the way that my friends care,
I like the way that my friends share,
Real friends.
I like the way we don't need to talk,
I like the way we laugh and walk.
Real friends.
I like that it's OK to be,

I like that they like me,
Real friends.
Real friends are there for me,
even when I forgot.
Real friends.
Forgot their birthday, forgot to phone,
Feeling safe and always at home.
Real friends.

Is it OK to disagree if you are a friend?
Most of my current friends are consistent and committed in their relating to me and to their other friends. But, there are times when an individual who we think of as 'a friend' isn't being very agreeable. When this happens we might think about them as not being very friendly. However, friendship doesn't mean always agreeing with the ideas, opinions and actions of our friends. Being a good companion might mean that we disagree or don't share our friend's interests, but that we can feel safe in saying this.

So, we might need to stop, think and process what is happening to us. This stops us acting too hastily. When we have worked out that we just have a differing viewpoint or perspective, then we can respond appropriately rather than react defensively. We are each allowed to have different perspectives. In fact we can celebrate this and use it to enrich our friendships. If we all liked the same things all of the time, life would be boring! I love science fiction but many of my good friends do not. At times my friends have chosen to come with me to see a film or watch a video just because they are my friends and want me to have their company, not because they necessarily like the movie.

Why do we have friends? Well we can choose to have friends because we like to share aspects of our lives with others. Then there are those times when having a friend helps us to carry the load that life brings to us. For example, decision-making can be tough at times. Gaining input from an objective source might make it a little easier. So, it can be helpful to share the ideas and thoughts that are involved with the decision-making process, for example Which ones...? What colour...? When shall...? and other such questions we might be asking ourselves or be asked of by others. The ultimate decision is still ours; we are simply exploring other views on the matter so that we can get a picture from all sides.

Even menial chores (gardening, spring cleaning, shopping) may seem less tiresome when shared with friends. Did you know that a team of husky dogs could pull a sleigh with quite a heavy load when the team all works together? A one-dog sleigh could not pull such a heavy load, so its owner would need to carry a less burdensome load and possibly work harder and longer to get the same amount of work done as an owner of a sleigh pulled by a team of dogs. In many situations having a friend to support and help out can lighten our load. You might have heard of the expression 'Many hands make light work'. This means that when we all work together the work gets done faster and is not so tedious. Of course reciprocity is the order of the day. This means that it works both ways. You help me and I help you.

But I'm no good at team work! If you find working, studying or just being in a group really difficult, you are not alone. So many of us find that trying to process 'group' information is very tiring, and the thought of working as a group is just too difficult. Maybe we need to delegate or distribute the activities to group members so we can still be part of the group without getting quickly worn out. For example, if I go shopping with a couple of friends, I suggest that we might like to separate and meet back at a particular place in an hour. If I need their opinion on a purchase, I can ask the store keeper to hold the item whilst I text my friends. My friends can then join me when they are ready and can pass on their comments to me about my proposed purchase. If I have a tendency to get lost (I do!) then I might need a guided tour of a place, before we separate, making sure I have the means to check in with the others if I need to.

 **I get confused and overloaded quickly.** Sometimes I need to explain to my friends that I'm not good at talking, walking and noticing where I'm going. It's better for me if I do one of these at a time and not all at once. Good friends are interested in our well-being and want us to be relaxed and not stressed. This means that they will accommodate any reasonable request from us. For example, I have a friend who can't tolerate perfume or jewellery on either herself or others. So, if I need to be in close contact with her (walking or talking with her), I don't wear these items.

Companionship, human or otherwise, can help put a different slant on life. When we are very excited and happy, we often want to share our fervour with others. I remember getting my first 'A' on an assignment. I was ecstatic! I stopped many of the other students who passed me in the hallways so I could share my joy with them. It made no sense to me when many of them shrugged their shoulders or didn't seem too enthusiastic about my grade.

Eventually I was able to talk this event over with a good friend. She explained to me, 'Not everyone will share your joy Wendy. Other students who didn't do as well as you might fail to celebrate with you because they might feel sad about their own grades.' Her words helped me to see that my behaviour could cause others to feel uncomfortable. It's not always a good thing to share one's excitement with everyone else. Instead, it might be wiser to share it with a close friend who will be able to rejoice with us. My difficulty is learning how to know who might be the right 'close' friend to share such moments with! We might need some practice with this. Sam, Josh and Emma illustrate this point.

Sam often came to stand close to me. Sometimes it was as if he were my shadow. Usually I didn't mind his closeness to me, but at times I wished he would let me be by myself or give me more room. Sam often echoed things I said and did. It felt as if he didn't have his own opinions and thoughts; at least if he did, he never shared them with me. Because Sam and I were in the same class-room frequently, we usually sat together. I liked the way Sam could draw pictures, especially cartoons. Although Sam was a close friend in many ways, and we shared time and space together, emotions and gathering 'meaning' from various events were diffi-cult for Sam. I concluded that Sam would find it hard to under-stand my concerns and was probably not the appropriate person to share my problems with. So, although this was my conclusion, Sam was no less a friend.

Josh was at the door again. 'Hello, Wendy,' he smiled and moved forward to give me a hug. I didn't mind hugs from Josh. His hugs were gentle but firm, not too long and recognisably part of his greeting to me. I hugged Josh back, with equal firmness and length of hold. 'Hi,' I said. Josh was not an infrequent visitor but he didn't presume upon my hospitality either. I always felt consid-ered and respected by him. Whenever Josh was going to come over he would ring me first to check that it was OK to call in. Josh was part of my study group for one of my Year 12 subjects. Josh and I had similar interests and could chat together about favourite topics for hours. He was an individual I could trust with a variety of concerns I had about school-work and related topics. I believed that Josh would be a firm friend to me, even after graduation from high school and even though I was older than him.

Emma was a fellow student at university. She had dreams. I loved being with Emma and enjoying the fellowship that comes with mutual understanding, shared interests and simply having fun together. I loved the way Emma played guitar and the passion she employed in her singing. For whatever reason I felt completely safe and at home with Emma. We could talk and laugh together well into the night. If I needed to talk to Emma, she was always available. Emma also shared her life and concerns with me. As the years have gone by Emma has remained a good friend and one I can share my innermost thoughts, concerns, dreams and desires with. It was Emma who helped me to understand the concept of friendship. Friends like Emma are the right kind of 'good' and 'close' friends who we can feel safe in sharing 'ourselves' (all of our joys and sorrows) with.

So, as you can see from the above, different friends bring different sentiments into each of our friendships. It's almost like we are different people with each one. Actually, I don't think we are different people so much as we are different sides of ourselves with different friends. One of my friends can draw laughter and spontaneity from me, another can help me focus upon what's necessary at that time, and so on. It's lovely to share different aspects of who we are with different friends.

Exclusive friendships. Some elements of some friendships are exclusive and quite intimate. Others are inclusive and less intimate. Then again, some friendships sit between the two or cross over from time to time between the both of them.

The friendships that are exclusive are usually of a romantic nature; for example, relationships that include marriage, or partnerships of a committed and sexual nature. These friendships will want each partner to spend the majority of their free time with the other, and some time with other friends, but not the most time. For a more detailed look at sexual and romantic relationships check out my book *Sex, Sexuality and the Autism Spectrum* (2005).

'Intimacy' is a word that conjures up a variety of images. When I asked a friend of mine what her understandings were of the word intimacy she said: 'Sharing, feeling safe, being close (physically and emotionally), sex, touch and being "one" with the other.' This sounds very much like the intimacy associated with exclusive relationships. Friendships can be intimate, but maybe they are intimate in different ways with different people. For example, sharing one's innermost thoughts and feelings is an intimate thing to do with a close friend or lover. Sharing a moment or a cuppa with a stranger can be intimate too. I don't know about you, but being next to someone for a long journey on a train, plane or bus can seem pretty intimate. Even though you might not share very deeply together or ever meet that person again! At times I have felt a deep and intimate connection with a character in a book I've been reading or in a film I've been watching. Intimacy can be transient and fleeting. It can also be deep and enduring. Understanding this is so has helped me cope with the lack of intimacy and the overwhelming emotions of transient intimacy that has swept over me at times I least expect it.

Other exclusive-type relationships may not be sexual or romantic but might mean doing special things with our special and closest friends. Sharing secrets, for example, is an activity we usually only share with friends we know and trust very well. Usually sharing our most intimate thoughts, dreams, desires and fears are things we do with very close friends. On occasion, we might need to tell some of these to a specialist, or a professional (doctor, social worker, psychologist, etc.) if, for example, we are engaged in counselling or some types of therapeutic intervention.

Inclusive friendships. I have a friend who had some work colleagues that she socialised with once a month. That is, once a month my friend and her colleagues met up to have a meal, go out to a movie or concert together. They didn't really spend time talking over the intimate details of their personal lives; they didn't talk or gossip about their families or other friends. The thing they enjoyed was each other's company in being out to various social functions. They talked about the movie they had watched or they talked about the meal they had eaten, but they didn't discuss politics or the state of the nation. Perhaps this type of a friendship can be thought of as *being part of a social group* and just being part of the 'gang'; some mates to hang out with. At times we might really enjoy doing light-hearted things; nothing too serious.

What if I need to talk about things? Then, at other times, we might feel the need to share things we feel quite deeply about. On such occasions we need to choose one person who we feel close to and can trust with our most inner feelings. Perhaps a good way to 'test' if the person we choose to talk deeply too is appropriate is to 'fish' for their comments on gossip. For example, you might ask the following types of questions:

- 'Do you like to know the gossip on others or do you prefer not to know?' If they prefer not to know and appear to you to be a friend who is a good listener, then your inner thoughts and feelings should be safe with them.

- 'I need to talk privately with you. Is this OK with you?' It's also a good idea that you voice your need to talk privately and let them know that what you need to share with them is for their ears only.

- 'If I tell you about things that are upsetting me, can I trust you to keep this information to yourself?' There are occasions when I need to let someone know, though, that if they tell me of plans or desires to hurt themselves or to hurt others, I might have to share that information with someone else (e.g. parents, doctor).

So, do we all need friends? This is a difficult question because by its nature it implies that we might not need other people in our lives. However, most of us will need other people but to varying degrees.

We are all different. Some people like to have lots of friends, and such individuals are usually very sociable by nature. They have outgoing personalities and are happiest when in the throng of activities with other people. Then there are others amongst us who are more introverted. This means that we like to visit social occasions on our terms for short amounts of time. We prefer a few friends rather than lots and like quieter occupations that appear less crowded.

At times, whatever our personality style, each of us might find ourselves needing to cross over our natural boundaries and inclinations to be part of a crowd (at a wedding, for example) or part of a smaller group than we would ordinarily choose. The good news is that as adults these propositions are quite reasonable and we are certainly within our rights to make our own choices. You might like to explore your personality type by taking the 'just for fun' personality test in Appendix 1.

When we are younger and still studying (at school, for example), the choices outlined above might be harder to access. For example, I found the usual classroom environment very diffi-cult. It was often noisy, cluttered and confusing. I wanted to have a friend but didn't know how to go about it. Academic study was hard enough to keep up with let alone the pursuit of friendship. I also wasn't very good at choosing likely candidates that I could trust and count on. Of course, each of us is allowed to 'want' to have a friend and allowed to not want to have a friend. But, even if we choose not to have a particular friend, we will still need to show ourselves to be friendly. You see, it will be difficult to encounter everyday life and avoid other people. So, we will need to decode the art of 'being' friendly and know how to practise it.

The following are some typical conversational openers, for when we want to be involved with another person.

- 'Hi, my name is…what's yours?'
- 'I really like…what about you?'
- 'I'm here today because…what about you?'
- 'Nice weather today, isn't it?'
- 'Rain again! I'm looking forward to some sunshine.'
- 'I haven't seen you here before, is this your first time?'

These conversational openers do not guarantee that the other person will want to get involved in a long conversation with us, they are just ways to be involved with another person briefly. These brief encounters may lead to longer conversations, but they also may simply serve to show we are friendly, and this helps to put the other person at ease. It's usually a good thing to feel at ease with someone else.

Good manners and being polite are all part of the 'being friendly' code. As such, we can use them for any occasion when we are around other people. I know at times I don't 'feel' like being friendly to someone else. I just want to get on with my business and move on. At such times it is OK to refrain from long conversations; perhaps a smile will suffice. If someone does ask us a question about how we are, then a brief answer like 'Well, thank you' and another smile will do, before we move on. If they persist with another question, it's OK to say, 'Can't stop to chat now; see you later.' Even if we think we might not see them later it's OK to use this expression. We won't be lying (even though it might feel uncomfortable); we are using well-known sayings that are generally accepted as a way to end a conversation and move on.

Are there some things we can share and do with some of our friends, but not with others? The short answer to this question is 'yes' there are. The difficulty is working out what to do with whom and when it needs to be exclusive. I use a formula to work this out. The formula is very simple: 'If in doubt, leave it out.' This means if I am not sure, then I don't do it. I also have developed specific patterns for certain relationships. This means that as a matter of routine I do certain things with certain people. For example, I used to jog with a certain friend, do the shopping with another friend, go to the footy with a different friend and work at my computer with another friend. The friend that shared computer time with me didn't like the footy, so this worked out well!

I have a couple of friends that I feel comfortable sharing a hot tub with (without my clothes on), but I wouldn't do this with all of my friends. Some of my friends would be embarrassed by nudity and others are OK with it. I need to check in with them and make sure that whatever I do in their company, they feel OK with.

I don't really like lots of 'touch' from people. On occasion it's OK, when someone arrives or leaves my company. But, there just are those individuals who are 'touchy-feely' people. They always have to touch you by putting their hand on your shoulder or arm or somewhere. I am confident that they believe this to be a good thing and don't do it to upset us. Therefore, I am happy to let them know that I'd rather they not touch me like this and, in fact, I can relate to them best when they don't stand too close to me. In order to accommodate their needs for touch I shake hands with them when they enter and leave my company.

Is our 'friend' a 'real' friend, someone who pretends to be a friend, or a person simply being friendly without intentions to develop an ongoing friendship? Unfortunately, there are some people who show themselves to be friendly but who don't actually have our interests at heart. This means, they might be friendly in order to get us to part with our money or other things they want from us. How can we know if their intentions are honourable? For example: A young man has just been paid and is happy to go down the pub with some mates. Whilst at the pub, one of 'the mates' says, 'You got paid today, John, great! You can buy us all a drink.' 'Yes,' says John. 'I do have money, I did get paid, I can buy the drinks.' This isn't a bad thing in itself, but if the mates only let John buy the drinks, use up all of his money and don't share the costs of buying the drinks between them, then they are not 'good' friends. They are only 'using' John to get drinks that they don't pay for. If they had John's best interests at heart, they would have shared the cost and paid for drinks for him as well.

Sometimes an individual is friendly to us but they might have an ulterior motive. Sales persons in shops who smile and are friendly do so because they want to put us at ease and be of assistance with any enquiries we might have concerning purchasable goods in their shop. Usually their smile is not a sign that they really like us, or they want to be our friend; they are just being friendly.

Then there are people who only want to use us for their personal gain or to get to other people. I find this type of interest really difficult to work out!

Real Friend?

You said you were my friend,
But your actions did not agree.
A real friend would offer more,
Not just words that don't see me.

You said you were my friend,
But then you failed to come.
Come over just to visit me,
Come over to just be.

Be here to be with me,
Even though it's hard.
Hard to know just what to say,
Hard to know just what to do?
A real friend would help me through.

Real friends hang in with you,
Even when it's rough.
They show interest just in you,
Not just in your stuff.

So if my list is too much for you,
I guess that says it all.
A real friend would do the lot,
My real friend, you are not!

Katy, below, is my daughter. Although Katy is a typical individual, she has chosen to pursue and understand her brothers in a

way that only a sibling of someone with autism and Asperger's can do. Life hasn't been easy for Katy (atypical parents and siblings, moving countries, losing friends, divorce, ill health) but she has come up trumps!

Friendship – The Katy way!

Friendship is a very complex term and there are so many views as to what makes a friend, least to say I have my views.

I consider true friends very rare and even harder to find, but when you do find one they add much value and meaning to your life. Many humans need to have people around them and I am no different. I love to have people around, but at the same time I often prefer the company of my pets. I find that in my pets I have the true meaning of a friend: they are loyal, loving and unconditional. All they want back is time spent with me, sitting at my feet or wanting a chest rub. They offer me comfort when I am sad and sense when I am unwell. My pets do not answer back and always forgive my impatience, never holding a grudge. In some ways an animal's love and friendship is similar to that of a child. Working with children, I see this everyday. At the end of a school day when the bell rings and parents are there to pick up their children, it touches me when I see the little ones run out and throw their arms around their parents and then chat eagerly about their day.

Throughout my life I have met and made many friends and lost some of the best friends I had. I am often the person who chases my friends, ringing them and organising to see them. At times I have found this hard to cope with, as I have felt let down and couldn't understand what I kept doing wrong. 'Why don't people want to be my friend? Why don't they put the same effort into the friendship as I do?' It was after being hurt by a friend that another friend of mine said to me, 'It is better to have loved and lost, than never to have loved at all.' This is how I now view friendships. I cannot change who I am or indeed make people like me, but I don't get as hurt as I used to because I remember that saying.

Another person who also helped me to realise that we can't make people like us was my mum. When I used to come home from school upset because some girls had picked on me, Mum used to say to me, 'It's their loss, darling, they don't know you and they are the ones missing out on you as their friend, because you are a very special person.' I thank my mum for those words because they have enabled me to deal with a lot of negativity I had to experience in my workplace, when I was teaching in the UK.

It is my nature that I see the good in people, that is not to say that I haven't learnt this, but rather that I choose to see the good. There is enough ugliness in the world today, and that is why I choose to see the little bit of good and I will always be polite and kind to those around. I also believe in treating others as you want to be treated; this is not always the case in life but it is again how I choose to live my life.

Friends are valuable and worthwhile, but they take time, effort, a lot of forgiveness and we each need to talk to the other. Sometimes with our friends we can tend to hold grudges and say that they should have known better. But have we been truly open with them? I know that with my life experience of friends that I can be guarded. Yes, I want friends and I want people to like me, but only a handful of true friends really know me. My best friends Georgina and husband Stu (apart from family) are the only two who truly know me and every facet of my personality. Sometimes in order to gain a friend we have to open up and show them who we are. Friends do come and go but just remember 'It is better to have LOVED and lost than never to have loved at all'. Friends help protect us against our leading a cold, lonely and unhappy existence.

In my eyes a true friend is one who is there for you when you least expect it; who does things for you just because they thought of you that day. They spend time with you, listening to you and learning from you. They are there to have fun with, cry with and just sit in silence with, if needs be. Friends give back what you put in.

All of my views have come about through watching one person, yes life experience has shaped my views but the main person who I have learnt from about friendship is my mother. Thanks, Mum, for being a great teacher – maybe the Aspie way of looking at friendship could open our eyes and teach us 'neurotypicals' how to be better friends. The Aspie way of friendship seems less complicated. Many Aspie individuals that I know do not care if you like them or not. But, they are loyal, unconditional with their love and want to spend time with you. Sometimes that may be through obsession, but their way still seems less complicated. I have watched my mum, my brothers, and children I work with, and this is the conclusion I have come to.

CHAPTER 2

How to Recognise a Friend from a Foe

At times we can think someone is a friend but then they disappoint us or let us down. Can they still be a friend if they do this? The answer might be 'yes'. It might not be their friendship which is in doubt so much as it might be a matter of communication. Communicating what we think and feel might make the difference between their understanding us and our feeling that they don't.

Let me explain. For a very long time I believed that other people knew what I was thinking, therefore there was no need to tell them. I now know that this isn't the case, that people need me to explain my thoughts, feelings and opinions, because otherwise they don't know them. The difficulty for many of us is that we may not have the words to explain or we may not actually know what we feel, think or believe in certain situations.

So, the first thing I need to do is to learn how to identify what I feel. At times this might mean learning to tell the difference between comfortable and uncomfortable. Then, as we take that knowledge a step further, we might be able to tell what aspect of a conversation or action we felt comfortable or uncomfortable about. I'm suggesting we might need to do some analysis and break things down a little, rather than try to master our emotions and consequent actions all at once.

What are comfortable feelings for you? Try this:

- Sit yourself down on a chair.
- Breathe in deeply, hold that breath for 3 seconds, breathe out.
- Notice what is happening to your chest as you breathe in and then out.
- Place your hands gently over your chest as you breathe. Is this a comfortable feeling for you or not? It shouldn't be uncomfortable, but breathing in and out to learn how to relax might take some practice.
- You might find that clenching your fists tight and then releasing them helps you to identify 'tight' and 'relaxed'.

What does 'relaxed' feel like for you? I can remember being told to 'relax and let it all go'. My problem at the time was that I didn't understand what these words meant – 'Let what go?' I thought. I needed to learn to let go of my stress and relax my body. Once we learn what it feels like to be physically comfortable and uncomfortable we might like to explore what emotional comfort or discomfort feel like. These feelings and understandings are very important. If we can't tell them apart, we might be vulnerable to being abused by others.

So, becoming aware of our bodies can help us to know when we are relaxed or when we feel stressed. Relaxed might be a comfortable feeling, being stressed is uncomfortable. When we are relaxed our breathing is steady, unbothered and flows naturally. When we are stressed our breathing may be more rapid, agitated and panicky.

Open them, close them… When they were young I used to sing a rhyme to my children using actions with my hands. It went like this: 'Open them, close them; open them, close them; open them, close them; give a little clap. Open them, close them; open them, close them; open them, close them; put them on your lap.' This rhyme helped the children to know what open and closed were (open hands, closed hands). It helped them take time to prepare to listen (hands on lap meant time to attend). It was a good way to prepare for what came next, and it helped them under-stand that it was time to stop one activity to get ready to move to another. In other words it created 'space' and gave them 'time' to check in with what was happening. I'm not suggesting that you need to sing this rhyme and do the actions, but it might be helpful to understand the principle behind the rhyme.

We each need time to 'feel' what is happening for us. It might mean we make this time by delaying our actions. 'I'll think about that and get back to you' is a reasonable answer if we are asked a question that we are unsure of the answer to. We do not have to reply right away, unless it's an emergency situation.

Is our discomfort a result of personality clash? I have learnt that some people put me at ease and are easy to be around. Other people do the opposite, and I feel a sense of discomfort around them. If this is happening for us, we then need to ask ourselves why we feel this discomfort. Is it physical, emotional or rela-tional? Does it happen because our personalities clash? Is it because we are too different from one another and don't have enough 'in common' to relate well and to share our interests?

There are many other variables and it's worth investigating. It might be that if we understand it, we can change the discomfort and make it go away. If it continues, however hard we try, we might need to accept our differences, keep our relating to a polite minimum and get on with other things. Outlined below are some basic explanations of personality styles and how they might impact upon our friendships.

Personality styles, learning and friendship

We all know that every person is unique and, as individuals, we each have our own 'style' of relating. However, there do seem to be some common threads in communication styles, expectations and interrelating intricacies that come from our learning styles, personalities and general interests. When we put all of this together and present it in the form of human behaviour it can be helpful in assisting us with understanding and managing our friendships. For example, if our learning style tends to be visual and we are extroverts we might be drawn to forming a friendship with someone who is outgoing, colourful, adventurous and exciting. If, however, we are extrovert but auditory learners we might be more drawn to someone who appears dynamic in conversation, but not flamboyant in their attire. At times it's as if visual blocks auditory or the other way around. So, if we are drawn to someone who is a mixture of the above, we might find our 'feelings' at odds with our thinking, which can cause conflict.

Learning styles

What is your learning style? Below are various learning styles that most of us fit into. Sometimes one style dominates our learning profile above another; at other times we might find ourselves a mixture of more than one.

Monotropic learners. This tends to describe those of us less typical individuals whose learning is guided by the means of single attention. We are not good at doing several things at once (outside of our interest system) and, if pushed to do so, become easily overloaded and reactive. It's as if our energy gets stuck in a bottleneck and we can't function. However, at times our focused attention can be a plus for us when our ability to attend to specific detail is useful.

Polytropic learners. This tends to describe those of us whose learning is guided by divided attention and who are able to attend to lots of different information at the same time (listening whilst looking and thinking whilst talking, etc.). Becoming overloaded and overwhelmed can happen, but, because energy flows easily in many directions, bottlenecking tends not to occur so rapidly. An individual with this disposition may be good at accommodating wider interests but energy used on this means decreased energy for the narrower attention tunnels.

These two umbrella terms relate in some capacity or other to most of us. These learning styles will dictate our primary occupation towards learning and will assist us in areas where each or the other is needed. The difficulty arises when one style is not understood and not catered for. This leads to denied access to learning and will disadvantage certain individuals.

In many situations it is assumed that all individuals have the capacity to function in similar ways. This is how society works out its societal norms. It's normal to do lots of things with lots of people and be governed by social priorities because most people do so. This argument fails to stand up to scrutiny, though, when one asks the right questions. For example, 'If all group activity depicts expected societal norms, what does this mean for "mass hysteria" or mass genocide?' Just because the majority, when in groups, are easily led into particular behaviours, it doesn't make all those behaviours acceptable or desirable.

Some non-group or individual behaviours have just as much right to exist as do those of a group. Those of us in minority groups have legitimate needs to access learning too. Once there was a time when left-handedness was seen as a handicap, and they tried to make all left-handed people write with their right hands. Once, being dyslexic was considered a handicap, now we use appropriate support and teaching methods to enable access to learning. Whether you are a monotropic or a polytropic learner – in the majority or the minority – you have a right to access learning and a right to be accommodated.

As well as being predisposed to being either polytropic or monotropic each of us has secondary learning styles that assist us with our learning. These are:

Visual learners:

- like to use visual materials like maps, charts, graphs, photos, etc.
- may like to 'see' people's faces and bodies so they can use the visual information coming from these sources to complement what they hear
- may like to use highlighters, underline words, and draw on pages to assist with memorising important points/facts
- are likely to take notes during lectures or ask teachers for handouts
- like to use think bubbles with drawings or 'clouds' linking up to illustrate brainstorming or ideas, before putting them into sequence or action
- might illustrate stories; use descriptive 'pictures' to explain concepts
- might relate well to computer, video, and other multi-media devices
- might prefer to study or read in quietness, away from verbal distractions

- enjoy illustrated books, comics and magazines, possibly choosing them over books, etc. that are not illustrated
- memorise information by picturing it in their head.

Auditory learners:
- may participate in discussions; usually around topics of interest
- lean towards making speeches and presentations
- prefer taping lectures rather than writing notes
- may email family and friends; even when in the same house
- may like to read text out loud or talk to themselves out loud during thinking or activities
- may create musical themes to aid memory; at times songs and music assist recall and learning
- like to discuss ideas; 'see' them out there via words
- dictate ideas as one speaks the words so as to 'hear' and 'see' how they fit together
- use verbal analogies and story to demonstrate points.

Tactile/kinaesthetic learners:
- may take frequent study breaks to employ physical exercise
- like to be on the move whilst learning, e.g. reading whilst in motion
- work whilst standing rather than sitting
- chew gum or eat lollies whilst studying
- use highlighters and colour coding to text
- feel the need to fill up work spaces with posters
- listen to music whilst studying
- skim through reading material to get the gist of the idea before deciding to read it more thoroughly.

The above particular learning styles frequently work in unison with each other. Most of us, although having one more dominant style, are mixtures of all. Also, as well as each of us having a particular learning style, we also have personality styles. The section below explores personality styles and how they might impact upon our friendships.

Personality styles

Personality styles have a big influence upon how we learn, what learning environments might suit us best and which people 'types' potentially make good friends for us. So, it's useful knowing which profile we each fit into and what this might mean for us as individuals. Of course, most of us tend to fit more than one profile or we have bits and pieces of different profiles. But, on the whole, we will be more predisposed to one profile above another.

There is much literature to suggest that our personalities change little over time. We inherit our personality dispositions and these are then complemented by our upbringing and our daily choices. For example, if we are prone to being negative, and our upbringing was inclined towards negative expectations, we might choose to believe that the world is a depressing place and not much good happens to us. If we are prone towards optimism, and our upbringing favoured a positive outlook, then we might be more inclined to expect that the world is a good place and good things will happen to us. Another way of thinking about this is to ask ourselves if we tend to see a cup of tea that isn't full as the cup half empty or the cup half full. The cup 'half empty' person might tend to view life through a window of negativity. The cup 'half full' person might tend to see life through a window of opportunity. I have a friend who thinks of kittens as 'full of fleas and vet bills', I have another friend who thinks of kittens as 'cuddly balls of fluff and fun'. It's not that one friend is right and the other is wrong, but how we view the world impacts upon our expectation of the world and of our friendships.

Extroversion and introversion. If you are an extrovert, you are probably outgoing and enjoy action. Extroverts are often lovers of parties, loud music, activity and constant happenings. They love to share their lives with other people and easily confide in friends or family. If you are an extrovert you might choose to focus upon study and work activities with the radio on or when surrounded by activity. It's as if your brain needs action in order to think. Sometimes, however, this can pose difficulties for us because we might like 'action' but only when we are in control. If the action is instigated by other people and we feel a sense of 'no control' then the activity might threaten our senses rather than enhance them.

If you are an introvert you probably prefer your own space rather than being amongst lots of people. For you to concentrate on study or thinking, you probably prefer the radio off and peaceful surroundings. You might find it hard to reach out easily to others and share your problems or difficulties with friends or family. Introverts think and function best when surrounded by calm, quiet and uncluttered space. However, there are times when we would value another person to share our space with, but on our terms only.

When we translate the above into impact upon friendship it might go something like this:

- **Extrovert:** Needs frequent conversations and interaction with friends. Enjoys social activities and thrives in busy, bustling environments. But, only as long as a sense of personal control and/or understanding accompany the action.

- **Introvert:** Needs less conversation time than the extrovert and more time to process information quietly. Also needs less activity time with others and more quiet time alone. At times would like to be joined by another but only when this is planned for and structured into a part of one's day.

- **Extrovert:** May find study time in groups with heaps of discussion aids learning. Therefore, finding friends from group activity might suit them well.

- **Introvert:** Some would say that introversion aids some forms of academic learning. For example, when one needs to pursue study at tertiary level that involves concepts and ideas outside of group study. Therefore, they might find friendship in individual contact over shared ideas, rather than from a gang, group or club activity.

Other aspects to personality. Whether you are an introverted person or an extroverted person is only one aspect of your personality profile. There are many other sides to one's personality. For example: Does intuition and sensing govern your 'view' of other people? Or do you use judgement and thinking? Perhaps you are guided by feeling? When one or the other of these personality traits tends to be our dominant receptor, it will impact upon our perception and involvement with our friends.

For example, if you are governed by your 'feelings' then you will tend to think that you are liked or well thought of only when you 'feel' good in someone's company. If you don't feel good, you might conclude that you are not liked or that your friend isn't interested in you. If you are governed by 'judging' you might judge too quickly or too harshly and not take the time to check in with what your friend meant or wanted from you.

The good news is that if we know our personality profile we can take stock of it in our relationships. I know that I am an introvert who tends towards thinking and intuition. I don't use sensing and feeling very much in my relationships. This means that I tend to be insensitive at times and I don't listen enough to my friends. Knowing my tendencies means that I can encourage my friends to make allowances for this and to let me know if they don't feel 'heard'. I also take stock of my involvement with friends and try to be more aware of their needs and less dictated to by my own dispositions. Try asking your friends if they are extrovert or introvert. You might like to share this chapter with them and even do some of the 'just for fun stuff' together.

Personality tests

There are many different personality tests, several of which can be found on the Internet. I have included some of my favourite websites and a 'just for fun' test, which you can do yourselves and with your friends, at the back of this book. Knowing one's personality and learning styles can be helpful in any of our relationships, but especially in our friendships.

This is important because it might be that an individual is not so much our enemy but rather they are so different from us, that we have nothing in common. So we might not have enough things in common to form a mutual friendship. Any successful friendship needs a foundation of mutual values, understanding, shared interests and enough similarity of concern that we can relate well through the inevitable ups and downs of life. There is a saying that 'opposites attract'. This might be true but the reality is that we need to be similar in lots of ways for any friendship to be mutual. If we are too opposite then we will encounter much conflict.

Friends test

The words below were sent to me on an email as one of those 'circulars' that folk pass around to one another. I don't usually take any notice of these and I delete them. However, I thought I'd include this one for you to read. I don't necessarily agree with it fully, but I can appreciate the sentiment behind it. When it says 'simple friend' it implies a person who might be less committed to the friendship than a 'real friend'. I don't actually think there is anything 'simple' about friendship. It seems to me that it can take quite a lot of hard work to maintain one's friendships!

A simple friend, when visiting, acts like a guest. A real friend opens your refrigerator and helps himself.

A simple friend has never seen you cry. A real friend has shoulders soggy from your tears.

A simple friend doesn't know your parents' first names. A real friend has their phone numbers in his address book.

A simple friend brings a bottle of wine to your party. A real friend comes early to help you cook and stays late to help you clean.

A simple friend hates it when you call after he has gone to bed. A real friend asks you why you took so long to call.

A simple friend seeks to talk with you about your problems. A real friend seeks to help you with your problems.

A simple friend wonders about your romantic history. A real friend could blackmail you with it.

A simple friend thinks the friendship is over when you have an argument. A real friend calls you after you had a fight.

A simple friend expects you to always be there for them. A real friend expects to always be there for you!

It's OK if you do not agree with all of the above; it's someone's idea of real friendship, but it's not everyone's idea. I think that the bottom line here is that a real friend aims to communicate in some depth with you and is not content to be superficial. They won't tire of relating to you, no matter what, and will hang on in there with you even when they don't want to!

When I first read the friendship test I thought to myself: 'I would think it rude if one of my friends just opened the fridge and helped themselves… I'd be OK about it if they checked in with me first or if I had already given them permission. I wouldn't want my friends to help me in the kitchen either; I prefer to be in that space cooking, on my own.' So, we are all different, and that's OK. The main thing is that we talk to each other about these things and don't take one another for granted.

* * *

What can we do if we want to be friends with someone who doesn't want to be our friend? There are a few scenarios here and we will explore them one at a time. First, sometimes an individual might want to be a friend but only for a season. Is this usual? I don't think we necessarily plan these things, but sometimes we meet someone during a holiday or whilst in hospital or some other 'transient' time. For that period we might share time, conversation and some activities, just like we would with any other friend. But this is just for a season, and we may not continue to relate to that person when that 'season' is over. Yes, this is usual and often very special.

This has happened to me on occasion, and such times have given me some very precious memories. I remember one time when I pursued a friendship after its 'season' had ended. It was very strange and the person I tried to relate to didn't seem to want to maintain the friendship with me. Their lives had moved on, so to speak, and mine had to. I needed to accept this and let go of that friendship. It didn't mean that what we shared wasn't real, but it did mean that its 'time' had ended and it was OK to move on.

Second, it might be that our friendship has gone stale. This means that our friendship isn't life-giving any more and we don't feel good in it. So, we might discover that in some people's company we feel depressed and we don't want to be their friend any more. The good news is that we don't usually have feelings in isolation. Maybe what we feel is mutual? Why not try to discuss this with your friend? Maybe they feel the same way too and they just don't know how to change it. At times doing 'fun' stuff together can be helpful. For example, you might like to take a short holiday together or go on an excursion to some place you haven't tried before. If you really can't come up with any ideas that you can agree on, it might be time to look for new friends to do things with. In many ways we should be open to the idea that new friends are always welcome in our lives. It doesn't mean we stop seeing our old friends (the friends we've had for the longer time) but that we start making space to discover new friends. You might find that having new friends brings vitality into your old friendships too.

Third, there are some people we would like to have as friends but who don't want to be our friends. It might be because they are already too busy or too committed with other things and don't have the time or the space. It might be that as individuals, we don't appear to fit their needs for a friend. Whatever it is, we need to respect their right to not be 'our friend'. The best way we can be their friend is to leave them alone.

Fourth, apart from the above, there are some people who actively don't like us or might even want to hurt us in some way. If this is your experience it might be best to leave such individuals to their own devices and get on with relating to those good people in your life, who have your best interests at heart.

What are the main characteristics that distinguish a friend from an enemy? Here is my list:

- A good and wise friend does not gossip to others about you (it might come back on them and cause embarrassment). *Enemies gossip and spread rumours about others as a tactic for hurting and upsetting people.*

- A good and wise friend finds the time to listen properly to what you are NOT saying. So they can help to support you in what you are really going through. This will work like cement between bricks and builds towards a good friendship. *Enemies take what you are not saying and use it against you. Rather than build you up it tears you down.*

- A good and wise friend accepts you for who you are and not who they think you should become. At the same time they don't leave you there but explore ways with you to develop potential and build the future positively.

- A good and wise friend knows 'what goes around comes around'. In other words they support you and you support them. The friendship is a giving relationship for you both. *Enemies take and do not give back. They are only interested in their own needs and not in yours.*

- A good and wise friend protects and nourishes the friendship so it will grow and develop and stay healthy. *Enemies are not interested in nurturing any friendship with you. They seek to rob you of opportunities and care only for their own interests.*

- A good and wise friend knows that the friendships they share are like precious jewels; to be treasured at all times.

What if I am being abused by a friend or family member?
No form of abuse (mental, physical, emotional or sexual) is ever OK. No one ever deserves to be abused or to be misused by someone else. If this is happening to you, it might be wise to tell someone about this rather than take matters into your own hands. If we don't act legitimately and lawfully over these matters it can mean we find ourselves involved with even worse situations (unemployment, the law). Recently there was a case where a young man with autism was killed by his mother. The court ruled that there was justification for the killing. This worries me. There are many individuals whose behaviour towards us can be

shocking and terribly abusive. However, if such behaviour comes from individuals who are lost, confused and terrified, we should be helping them find their way and teaching them how to deal with their fears, so we can get rid of their fears rather than getting rid of the individuals! This is not written out of harsh judgement and no concern for the family circumstances, but it is posted as a concern that the right messages get out into public places. Seek help and shout loudly so someone listens to you, don't take matters into your own hands.

Friends

Friends always stay close beside you,
Friends ride the glad and the sad.
Memories shared with my good friends,
Will keep me through times good and bad.

Friends are our richest resource,
Friends walk through day and through night.
Life with our friends is the best course,
As friends we each play our true part.

Friends always stay close beside you,
Friends ride the glad and the sad.
Memories shared with my good friends,
Will keep me through times good and bad.

A truer friend had no one,
As you my dear friend are to me.
I will be true to our friendship,
As true as a true friend can be.

Friends always stay close beside you,
Friends ride the glad and the sad.
Memories shared with my good friends,
Will keep me through times good and bad.

Some thoughts on friendship (by Janet Pett and Jill Godwin)

When does a friendship start? We have been friends with Wendy and Beatrice for 12 years. We first met Wendy in the context of shared experiences of marginalisation – as gays in the Christian world and Christians in the gay world. Initially we maintained a connection with Wendy and Beatrice out of our need for solidarity. We noticed some of Wendy's puzzling ways, but these didn't seem as important as the things we had in common – like rejection by people dear to us, and important to us. (Janet: In truth it was Jill who encouraged me to be accepting of Wendy. I'm a conforming kind of person who would like just to blend into the background. Jill is much more understanding of eccentricity and difference.)

Janet Pett and Jill Godwin

When mutual acquaintances warned us that Wendy was a manipulative person who might take advantage of us, we felt disappointed by them rather than by Wendy – partly because it seemed then that their acceptance of *us* had depended on our being as *normal* as possible.

Friendship kind of grew on us, as we discovered other mutual interests, like bird watching and walking by the sea. We don't have to see each other often to enjoy a deep connection, strengthened by the highs and lows of life we have all experienced. We look back now, with pleasure and gratitude, on a shared history.

When Wendy announced her Aspie diagnosis, it was a resounding AHA! moment. Suddenly everything made sense. In retrospect, the incidents which had caused some people to mistrust Wendy were obvious misunderstandings. Knowing Wendy has taught us so much about the world and about ourselves.

Some hints for neurotypical friends of Aspies

- Be specific about arrangements. Don't change dates and times without considering what this may mean for your friend.

- Be specific about your commitment. Don't offer what you don't intend to deliver. This common, and socially acceptable, form of lying is very confusing for the literally minded.

- Be explicit about the difference between gifts and loans. Your Aspie friends will not be offended if you spell it out.

- Think about whether your wording may be misunderstood. I once asked Wendy to *watch the door for me*. I meant her to tell me when another friend had arrived, but when I returned an hour later, Wendy was still anxiously watching the door.

- Keep in touch in few words. Email is great. Wendy can email you in the middle of the night and you can reply at your leisure.

- Keep your advice until your friend asks for it. But be prepared to explain the conventions of new situations.

Often when you analyse a situation for your Aspie friend you realise how ridiculous some conventions are; e.g. how silly is it that a woman is expected to dress *up* to go out in the evening, but her male partner can wear his gardening clothes if they are clean?

- Let your friend organise his or her own food. If you're eating out, choose a place where individual preferences can be accommodated. Food courts are good at very quiet times.

- If you really have to share dishes, let an Aspie order. It's more likely that you can eat their food (arranged by size or shape or colour or touching or not touching or whatever) than they can eat yours.

- When dining out with your Aspie friends, try to see unusual requirements as an opportunity for the management to deliver superior service. I used to be embarrassed when Wendy questioned a waiter about ingredients, but eventually I noticed that often the staff felt happy if they really pleased their customers. If they don't, go somewhere else. We recommend a Chinese takeaway place to all our friends because they cheerfully accommodate Wendy's wishes.

- Enjoy the fact that your Aspie friend will say if he or she does not like something. This saves a lot of trouble guessing what a person really thinks, or doesn't think – or is not even thinking about.

- Be happy if your friend cares not for the latest fashions. We love the way Wendy and Beatrice love us whatever we are wearing.

- If people stare at you and your friends, smile happily at the starers. I've tried staring back, but this usually just makes me feel cross. Smiling feels good.

- And remember whenever people stare at you, that some of them are wishing they had the courage to be like you.

Hints for Aspies

- Show interest in your friend's concerns. Even friends who only meet over a shared task take a little interest in each other's lives. *How was your weekend? Did your daughter get her car fixed? Is your broken foot still troubling you? How is your elderly mother?* are a few examples of the type of thing people might say to one another.

- You don't need to have a conversation; just a few words will do: *Hmm, I'm sorry to hear that there's been no improvement.* OR *You must be relieved about that.*

- You never know, this may lead to another mutual interest you didn't know you had.

In the company of Wendy and Beatrice, we enjoy a special freedom to be ourselves. As friends of long standing, we care about each other and for each other. We forgive each other for offence or upset we have unintentionally caused. And we encourage each other to keep on working towards peace and understanding between people of all kinds.

CHAPTER 3

Too Many Friends!

Can a person have too many friends? I can remember thinking, 'Well, I guess I have my quota of friends now.' Actually, I don't think one can really have too many friends, but if one had lots of friends it might take a bit of juggling to keep them all happy! Are there moments when you don't want the phone to ring?

I have 'friends' of varying degrees (different levels of friendship from slightly superficial to full-on intimate) all around the world. The problem is that I can't just 'pop' in and have a cup of tea with them when they might live in a different country to me. I can usually keep in touch via email, and this is truly a great medium for me, but there are times when I would like to see and spend time with them in person. I take what time I can access and always appreciate their making the time for me too. Sometimes, perhaps because we don't get to catch up that often, it's all the more special when we can.

What does it mean to be considerate? I remember getting into trouble over the issue of timing with one of my friends. I'm not a good sleeper and I was having a rough time one night (feeling upset and anxious) so I telephoned her. It was 3am and I woke her up. She wasn't pleased with me. She said that when one cared for others they would understand that it was a bad idea to phone them in the middle of the night, unless it was an emergency. It certainly felt like an emergency to me! However, I took this on board and aimed to deal with my anxiety differently next time. These days I write emails to my friends in different countries. I also find that writing things down, so I can discuss them at an appropriate time, is quite useful. It gives me some processing time and I often feel better too. Just writing about things, rather than talking about them straight away, can help give me a clearer perspective on the situation. When I react too quickly, without processing it first, I often react in haste; and at times this leads to an unhelpful response. I don't like the delay, I much prefer instant gratification, but it's usually worth my holding off a while.

I'm an 'instant' type of person. I react first and think later! I find it very hard to think clearly if my emotions are all fired up. However, telling myself to take the time to cool off and calm down is often a good course of action. Go for a walk; do some writing; if it's appropriate, talk about things to someone else and generally try to put some space between my emotions and the incident; these are all good choices.

New friends? Once when we moved house I thought that it would be very difficult to make (find) some new friends. I was invited to morning tea with a neighbour. They introduced me to the other neighbours and some of their friends. As I watched the people interact with each other, it seemed obvious that they were all friends with one another and, after the initial introductions, I was left out in the cold (felt ignored) as they chatted and laughed together. I remember thinking, 'They have their friends; there isn't any room for another friend. I'm too late.' Well, I think my thinking on this was inaccurate. This kind of thinking happened to me at school too. Because my family moved around a lot I often joined a school after a term had started. This meant that it was hard to break into 'the friendship scene' because the other children were sorted about who their friends were. This might be a relevant consideration for when we are children, but I don't think it should apply to us as adults. For adults the rules are different. Being more grown up and mature should mean we can work out our time and be more inclusive of others as we meet them. There are lots of potential new friends out there waiting to be discovered!

What would be the ideal number of people to have as one's friends? I guess this will mean different things for different people. That is, some of us are happy to have fewer friends, and some are happy to have more friends than others. Really, there isn't an ideal number; we just have as many friends as we can relate to at any given time.

If our friends get 'too much' at times, then it's fine to let them know how we are feeling. I love my friends, but I relate best to them one at a time. I can cope with a small group of friends but not too many. If I am invited to a party, then I try to remember that it's OK to go for a short time and I might not get to talk to any one person in any real depth. The conversation is allowed to be superficial at parties. Sometimes, when I stand alone, someone will chat to me and try to relate to me at a more meaningful level. This is OK too.

Do friends 'change' over time, as people? If they do, what should one do if one doesn't like or agree with the changes? As individuals we are all likely to change over time. We might change in our physical appearance by getting taller, slimmer, fatter or balder. We might change our hair style and even hair colour. I remember being very upset when one of my friends changed her hair style. She just didn't look like 'her' any more and I felt very uncomfortable. I felt so bad that I was cross with her for doing this. It almost felt like she was making me feel bad by her actions. I now know that no one can 'make' us feel bad. The feeling comes from our response to a situation, often outside of our control. These days I've learnt (mostly) to let the discomfort go. If people make choices I don't agree with (unless it's unjust or abusive) I can tell myself it's their decision and I don't need to do anything about it. Learning to 'shrug' and say 'Oh well' is very useful, and I employ this quite often.

As we gain more understanding and insight into our world, and the world of others, it is inevitable that we will change. We might change our views and beliefs. We might change our attitudes and values. Once there was a time when my beliefs were 'black and white'; this means I held very strong beliefs which were not very accommodating of any belief that was different to mine. Now, I am more 'open' to the idea that people will not always share my beliefs, and this is OK. I might feel uncomfortable about this, but this is my problem not theirs.

I Believe

I believe life is for living,
But sometimes death occurs.
I believe there is a purpose,
For each of us on earth.

I believe that sometimes,
What I believe must go.
To have you as my friend,
Might mean knowing what you know.

'Seeing is believing,'
My friend says with glee.
I answer him with smiley grin,
'Believing is seeing. Walk a while with me.

'Take my hand across this land,
Discover the treasure ahead.
It's not all that glitters, helps us stand,
True friendship is gold; a jewel instead.

'For friendship says "I believe in you",
This is true treasure indeed.
I have you and you have me.
Together we learn what it means to be free.'

So, learning to 'pick our battles' and let go of things that really are not important, in the overall scheme of things, will mean that disagreements can be minimal. Change is inevitable, we'd best accept it.

OK, I can see the value of this, but how will we know if the kind of change our friendship is experiencing is unhelpful? I think I have three main questions/rules about this. If the change fits in with these questions/rules I accept it; if it does not, I challenge it. My three questions/rules are:

• Does this change have the potential to strengthen our friendship?

• Is this change being made with my friend's best interest at heart?

• Will this change be good for our personal growth and development?

You see, I might not like the changes my friendships may go through (friends may move and be less accessible; I may have to share them with other friends and commitments; they might be unwell or incapacitated and not as available to me as I would like, etc.). All of the above have the potential to deepen one's friendships. However, if the change to my friendships potentially threatens the health of the friendship, or is not in the best interest of the individual and might cause stagnation, then I query it and encourage discussion on the matter. Friendship is a very precious state between people and should never be taken for granted.

What does 'unconditional love' mean? Could it mean different things to different people? Unconditional love implies a kind of love that is selfless and freely given. It is not self-effacing, nor does it lie down in order to become an endless doormat. It might be differently understood in the light of one's values or traditions. My dog 'loves' me unconditionally and accepts me as her hero no matter how I treat her. This type of unconditional love is great, in a dog! If we have a friend who constantly puts themselves down in order to raise another up, then I question their motive. Maybe their self-esteem and confidence are low? If this is the case, then maybe I have a duty, as a friend, to challenge their behaviour and their thinking. I reckon we can get into a rut and not realise we are doing this. There was a time in my life where I apologised if someone opened the door and bumped into me. Eventually a friend noticed and commented that I walked with my face turned towards the ground and seemed to apologise for my existence. She encouraged me to walk tall, hold my head up and face the world with confidence. I didn't feel very confident, but I chose to act as if I were. This is a case of 'you have to fake it to make it'.

The right kind of 'unconditional love' lets the loved one be themselves and does not try to change them. It hopes for the best for that friend and finds value and appreciation in the smallest of things that they do. It hardly notices faults and flaws, but seeks only to encourage and honour the individual or person. This is the kind of love I want to receive and the kind of love I want to give.

Is it OK to want to share some things with our friends, but not everything? Yes it is. In fact, it's probably vital to the health and prosperity of our friendships. We need to share good times and bad times together, but not to harp on about them obsessively.

Of course, there are some things our friends do not need to know. I try to vet my conversations with my friends so that I share the gist of things but not all of the detail. I want my friends to get the picture I am giving them, but I don't want them to drown in it!

What about money? Should we lend money to our friends? Should we lend our friends anything at all; or should we give freely and not expect our things to be returned? These are difficult questions, and I have heard it said that one should never lend money to one's friends because if they fail to pay it back it can be seen as a sign of poor friendship. I have lent money and other things to friends. Sometimes I have been repaid and my goods have been returned, other times I have not.

This can certainly be a point of conflict. These days I do one of two things. When I lend something I aim to make a note of it, fix a date for its return and let my friend know that it is only a loan and there is a time limit to it. If they agree to these conditions, then they shouldn't be upset if I remind them of this. Having a clear, perhaps written, agreement is helpful.

If we always just give to our friends, they might not respect us and will tend to believe that we are a bottomless pit! Usually, none of us can keep giving without getting back in return. This doesn't just apply to material things but it also applies to emotional and physical support.

Misconception. One friend I had was very insistent that he was happy to help me with my computing needs. I had a new computer and, at that time, wasn't computer literate. The first few times I called him he was happy to oblige. However, over time his attitude changed towards me. After a while he withdrew his friendship. I didn't understand what had happened and I talked to our mutual friend. He explained that this friend was willing to support me, but to a limit. He had felt used and had believed that I only valued him for what he could do for me. I was shocked to hear this and very sad too. In my usual way I had taken my friend's offer literally and had believed him when he had said 'call me at any time'. Today I am a little wiser and I try to make sure my friends don't feel taken for granted!

So, how can we be sure our friends are being truthful? It is quite likely that our friends will do their utmost to be truthful. But, there will be those occasions when they believe it to be better not to be truly honest with us. Maybe they feel unwell, but, when asked, they might say that they are fine. They do this to save us the feelings of concern that might burden us. Perhaps they believe that they will recover fast and there is no need to bother us with their concerns. Then there are other times when it seems more considerate to spare us the reality of a situation. Again, when asked, they might respond as if all is well, even if it isn't. Perhaps personal pride plays a role here, or people are governed by the need to appear in control of their lives, even if they feel that they are not!

I'm Smiling

You look at me, I smile at you.
My smile hides my pain.
I'd like to tell you how I feel,
To let you know my smile's not real.
But then I'd have to feel again.
Feel again the loss,
Feel again the cost.
Feel again, feel again.

If only this grief would go.
If only I could let you know.
If only, if only.

I have been in this position myself. A place of pain where I felt I had to carry it all on my own. Some things just feel too difficult to share. Maybe they are best kept unsaid, or maybe if we had the courage we could share them and experience some relief. I don't think there is a standard answer here, it isn't one-size-fits-all. At times we will find the strength to share our load with a friend; at other times it will be a quietly whispered prayer that none can hear save the Almighty.

'Computers don't have feelings, so it's much easier for me to share my problems over the net.'

'If we don't share our pain and problems, how will we experience the care shown to us by another?'

'When we go out of our way to visit a friend, it helps us to look up and not always down at ourselves.'

'We may not know our future, but our future can be shared with our friends.'

'Sometimes knowing how to be a good friend will mean we have to play the role of detective. We need to watch for clues of how our friend feels, so we can work out what they need from us.'

Having and being friends (by Katy Harris)

I am lucky because when I was at school I had a lot of confidence and so making friends with people was easy for me, and because I was quite open and talkative people were easily drawn to me. That experience really helps me in adult life. Now I am not as confident, but remembering that I am a person that once easily had friends helps me to try to talk to people as though I was the chatty person that never thought twice about how I presented myself to the world. So 'faking' the ability to show great interest and engagement with people, whilst feeling a little obvious at first,

Katy Harris (left), seen here with myself and Beatrice, is a friend who slipped into my life via mutual colleagues and whose home and heart are always open to me

really helps me get to know people until I become comfortable enough to just be myself.

I need this because I don't live in my country of origin, and the city where I stay has lots of people who live here for just a year or two (I am an occupational therapist in Singapore). If I don't try to make new friends and my old friends leave here then I start to feel very sad and despondent about making relationships with people. So even when I have good friends, I still have to make an effort to meet new people and include them in my life so that I have a new store of people to make connections with when older friends move away. It sounds a bit calculating, but it is just the way things are in my society for adults and for children. In the world today there is so much change that it is good to try not to rely too heavily on one person.

Fortunately I meet a lot of new people, and because they have moved to this city they too want to make new friends. At first I used to be friends with anyone who wanted to be friends with me, but I found that I ended up being friends with people who some-times made my life difficult because they were too bossy or too needy. Now I try to be nice to that type of person when we meet, but I am cautious about making future arrangements to meet up. On the other hand, when I do meet people I genuinely like and find interesting, I have to remind myself to pursue them and follow it up with a call to see if they'd like to get together. Some-times it works out and sometimes not, and I try to be relaxed about either outcome.

However, having said that, I often find that people come into my life whom I don't actively choose – it just happens. Initially whilst I am with them I occasionally think 'but you are not my type of person' and then, strangely, for one reason or another, I am useful to them or they to me. I wonder if there is a universal matchmaker somewhere which allows people to drift towards those who are supposed to point them along in their path of life?

I like having friends and can't imagine life without them, but I get tired dealing with them sometimes. I think many people like the idea of friends but find that arranging to meet and making it evident that you care can get a bit tricky in a busy world. I get frus-trated by feeling that I have to keep in touch and call or email often, but when I see them, I almost always feel I have enjoyed the experience. Talking away to a friend over coffee or lunch makes me feel cared for and connected, gives me ideas to think about and makes me feel it's OK to share my life and theirs, give opinions and share enjoyments. I also like 'doing things' with friends, things like going for a walk or a movie, because doing these things alone provides only half the value – the other half comes in talking about the experience and the feelings and having them listened to and commented on by another.

So, I have friendships which are old, and there is no sense of 'working at' them – they just keep going; I have medium-term friendships where we are still discovering things about one another, but mostly just sharing time and care; and newer friend-ships where there is a little more caution and need to respect boundaries, but more energy and excitement. I am lucky, but I do have to put some effort in myself to see a return. I am never going to be the sort of person who does all that without some sense of 'trying'. Fortunately I have become my own friend as I have grown through life, which is also very valuable!

A friendship ring put together by my friend Katy Harris. Each symbol represents a specific friendship, and the patterned line represents the links and type of relationship experienced by Katy and each of her particular friendship styles.

The ring drawn above represents some of my friendships. When I see this I can get a better picture of how close I feel with people and why I like them. I use symbols to indicate what my friends mean to me:

> The sun – warm, positive, always there even on cloudy
>   days
> Square heart – solid, practical and kind
> Beach ball – fun and light
> Weights – strong, capable, sometimes heavy
> Candle – sometimes light but sometimes very spent

Diamond – multi-faceted, reflects back, precious
Outstretched hand – helpful, but black and white not a
   feeler
Lotus sitter – yoga friend who is seeking peace
Dynamite – explosive and loud

Lines represent the strength and type of my connection to my friends:

A bold line shows a strong link.
A broken line indicates that the friendship is on and off
   but rewarding.
A dotted line means we give and share when we can.
A wavy line shows easy but not frequent friendship.
And the zig-zag is a little dangerous.

★ ★ ★

You might like to think about how you could represent your own friendships in a diagram. Drawing different types of lines between us and our friends can symbolically represent how we relate. Such a diagram, like Katy's above, might help us to see more clearly the type of friendships we have and the journey we are on together.

CHAPTER 4

You're Just Too Honest!

Honesty is a matter of debate. Sometimes I'm more honest when I am dishonest! Let me explain. There was this time when I called over to visit with a friend. I exclaimed how pleased I was to see her and how I really enjoyed her company. My friend said, 'You're too honest.' Which was a way of saying 'You're too kind'. She didn't really mean it the way I took it though. I thought she was teasing me and was suggesting that I was a bit over the top in my responses. In fact, my honesty had caused her to feel uncomfortable, and she would have coped better if I had said 'Oh no, it's yourself again is it' or something like this. An exclamation of negative proportion with a positive twist! I don't know why some people have problems with affirmation, but if they do I try to accommodate them.

Friends should be honest with each other. But what does this mean? In a real friendship where trust and safety are a given, maybe the word 'should' is null and void? I mean, one doesn't need to feel that one 'should' about anything. The sense of obligation to one another is replaced by 'it's my pleasure to do this; you are my friend'. I remember a song from my youth. There were words in it that took a bit of working out for me '...he ain't heavy; he's my brother'. I used to think these words were strange because I have a brother and he is much heavier than me! You see, the words are not meant to be taken literally, but symbolically. When you are with your friends it's not a chore to help them, not heavy burdensome work, but it is an honour and a joy. So, a good friend can rest in the assurance of another's friendship.

Honest communication or welcomed dishonesty? There are times when conversation hides the reality of a sad situation or when one expresses a smile but feels disappointed. Friends try to cover for each other, and this might mean allowing your friend to bury their grief until such a time when they are willing to look at it. It might 'feel' like they are being dishonest when they 'pretend' that all is well, but pretending buys them some time until they can deal with the things going on for them.

When my son was killed I swung into action mode. I organised the celebration of his life, contacted friends and family, constantly checked in with the police to check out how the investigation of Mattie's death was going and spoke frequently to the Coroner's Office, so I was fully informed of all investigations. I was obsessed with organising and arranging whatever was needed. I created a photo album with fun captions, so we had a book of remembrance that explored Mattie's very full life of 19 years. There was no time to grieve! I didn't cry for several weeks. I felt numb. I also felt guilty for this non-expression of sadness. When my friends and my other children cried, I comforted them. Eventually, when there was time and nothing needed to be organised, I cried. I am grateful to my friends who supported me at that time. They knew I needed time.

Although I felt as if I were 'lying' when people said how sad it was (because I felt numb) and I agreed with them, I now know that one can agree with sentiment without having to share the emotions. This is especially true when emotional energy is being used up somewhere else.

What if my being honest causes my friend to suffer? Maybe I need to learn when to keep quiet about something and when to speak my mind. Yes, we all do. This is quite a difficult thing to work out though. What I tend to do is be a detective and look out for the signs. Some of the signs to look out for are:

- Does my friend seem 'happy and comfortable' to talk about this topic or do they shy away from it? If it feels like you have to 'pull' the information from them and they seem unwilling to talk about it at this time, you might need to give them some time and approach the subject later.

- When will I know what is later? Again, I look for the signs that say 'I'm ready to talk' from my friend.

- When friends talk I need to listen and not pass judgement. I often find this the hardest thing to do!

- Then there will be those times when I might think something or know something that isn't necessary to pass on to my friend. I need to think, 'Do they need to know this? Will sharing this information cause my friend pain or pleasure?' If the answer is 'pain', I should think carefully and possibly decide not to tell them.

- Then again, as one friend said to me, 'I'm allowed to be upset, Wendy. This is not a good reason not to tell me.' So, there will also be times when a friend needs to hear what you need to say, even though it's uncomfortable. I'm still working this one out!

There will be times when my friend chooses to visit with or spend time with a different friend. Does this mean that they are not my friend any more? No, it doesn't mean this. It means that friends share the company of others and sometimes we will spend individual time with a variety of people, sometimes we spend time in groups. I am no less important to my friends because I spend time with others, and they are no less important to me when they are with other people and not with me. My feelings may try to tell me that this is so, but sometimes our feelings lie!

Feelings change like the wind and cannot be relied upon. What we need to look at is 'the evidence' to support what we feel. For example, if I think, 'I am not important to my friend. If I were important then they would be here with me and would not be somewhere else', I can answer this belief with another statement. The statement might say something like this: 'Where is the evidence for this thinking?' 'Why did you feel important to your friend in the past?' 'Are you only important in their company, or could it be that you are important just because you are?' 'Is your friend important to you whether they are with you or not?' You see, our feelings are very strong and at times they can capture our thinking and dominate it. This can be a useful thing, but it can also be misleading. Learning to challenge our thinking and not be ruled by our feelings can take a bit of work; but if we manage it, then we are less likely to be slaves to our feelings and thought processes.

Got to fake it to make it! Another example of how inadequate feelings can be is demonstrated by the following. At times, when I am far away from my friends, I don't 'feel' very close to them. Usually my feelings are because of the distance and my being pre-occupied with other things. If we felt intense emotion all of the time we would be quickly worn out! It's a better thing to 'act' as if we felt close, felt loved, felt loyal, and so on, rather than wait for the accompanying emotion. Then, quite often, the feelings follow on from our actions. If they don't, it might simply be that we don't have the energy connection at this time, it may come later. Even if it doesn't come later, it's still OK. The issue is that it is always good to act in a loving, supportive manner, in spite of how we feel. In the past this was difficult for me because if I didn't 'feel' it then I didn't do it. If the emotion was absent, I felt as if I were lying if I acted as if it were present. Now, I have a broader understanding and I appreciate how emotions and feelings are not always based in reality and are not to be trusted. These days I weigh up the evidence!

How can I know about sharing friendship and about letting go of others so they can 'do their own thing'? There are moments when we each want time to ourselves. This is usual and a very healthy thing. I need to be on my own to 'think' things through, or to work something out. When I am in company it's not so easy to process things that are happening. However, knowing the right time to be on our own and the right time to be with one's friends is difficult.

Things we can do:

- Check in with them if they need time to themselves.
- Check in with myself: Do I need time to myself?
- Check in to see if we are expecting the same thing (or if we have different expectations).
- Try not to assume anything, but ask questions so we can check we are thinking the same way.
- Respect the other person and their decisions.

Being adults is good because we get to make grown-up decisions. Grown-up decisions are based upon understanding and wisdom. Therefore, learning how to share one's friends and give them time is a very grown-up thing to do. I like the way this makes me feel. If I am mean and childish with my friendships and not good at sharing, I actually feel uncomfortable and I don't like the feeling at all!

What is personal autonomy? How can I tell if I have it? Personal autonomy means that your sense of self is intact (i.e. you know what you like, think, feel, etc. and don't find it difficult to process most decisions within a reasonable time). With this sense of self comes confidence in things like: decision making, relationships, navigating emotions and trusting in one's own abilities and judgements.

However, having said this, I do think personal autonomy is liable to change according to the stresses and strains one is experiencing. For example, if one is unwell and being ill is dominating your time and energy, then your decision-making abilities might be impaired. If you are overloaded and feeling confused you might not be too good at navigating a supermarket or university campus! This has less to do with autonomy than it does with a lack of resources available to you at the time.

Personal autonomy is quite an important feature for successful relationships. If we want to avoid co-dependency, misunderstanding, 'needy piggy' syndrome and a general urge to 'leave it to beaver', then we need a good sense of autonomy. If you are finding that your friendships seem a bit one-sided, or that the people you thought of as friends were constantly making decisions for you and not with you, it might be because you give out signals of being someone with poor autonomy.

Someone who is unsure and ill-equipped, however, is not always a person of poor autonomy. It might just be that the environment isn't suited to their needs and, therefore, is making it difficult for them to read and process information, and then act upon it accordingly. For example, if a person presents with visual impairment and cannot 'see' via conventional means, they need to be provided with the means to navigate their lives in a way that suits them (guide dog; Braille; talking books, etc.). So it is for many of us on the ASD spectrum…we need time.

The above type of example can apply to other situations too. For many of us on the autistic spectrum, our need for time to process information, and then even more time to enact any kind of decision process, is almost mandatory. We are often not too good at speedy decisions. If we do make hasty decisions due to time or people pressure, they may not be the decisions we would make if given the time we need.

Saying what we mean; meaning what we say? For friendships, perceptions and words could mean some disastrous outcomes. For example, in my relationship with one of my Aspie friends (we are both quite literal) I have been disappointed often and have even begun to think they were doing 'this' to me on purpose! My friend would agree to an outing with me, that I suggested. I would turn up prepared to go out with her and she would then say, 'Oh, I don't want to do this.' To me it seemed that she was always changing her mind! However, after this happening frequently over many years, we talked together about it. We worked out that she was often saying 'Yes' to something because it was easier than saying 'No'. I explained how disappointed I was constantly, and that this was causing me to experience feelings of mistrust and withdrawal from her. The solution was an easy one, albeit not that simple to put into practice for me (I'm not good at delaying gratification). I just needed to give her more time and not expect an answer on the spot!

So you see, sharing time with friends; understanding their need to share time with different friends apart from us; allowing 'time' in order to process arrangements; and appreciating what, when and where honesty is appropriate are all essential ingredients for successful friendships.

Success

Success is a very strange thing,
Sometimes it is welcome,
Sometimes it is not.
Sometimes I like remembering,
Sometimes I'm glad I forgot.
Sometimes it feels wonderful,
Sometimes it does not.
Success for you,
Success for me,
Success is learning how to be.

CHAPTER 5

Family Comes First?

 **Relationships are important but some relationships seem to have more importance than others. How can I tell which ones are which?** This is a tricky question. Maybe there is no one answer but many. For example, my children are always important to me, nothing can ever change that. But, there are occasions when my attention is taken up by other relationships. Giving my attention to others and not my children does not mean that my children are less important. It does mean that another matter needs my attention at this time. So, it's not an issue of who is or who is not important to me, so much as 'what's important or what's requiring my attention at this time?'. This distinction, between *who* and *what*, is a very important one and I am still working on understanding this.

Then there are those relationships that by their very nature say that they are more important than some others. Usually romantic relationships take precedence over non-romantic relationships. So, husband and wife, or partner to partner, are a priority. A mother to child relationship takes precedence over a mother and friend relationship. This is by necessity because children are dependent upon their parents whilst grown-ups are usually independent and, therefore, don't usually require such an in-depth degree of supervision, as mother to child might.

When I have times of feeling unimportant to a friend, because their attention is occupied, I try to check in and just ask myself, 'Is this an occasion of *what* is important and not *who*?' If my answer is, 'Yes, this is an occasion of *what* of importance needs to happen', then it helps me to appreciate that sometimes situations and circumstances take priority for action, but not priority over friendships. So, I need to learn to tell my feelings that they are misinformed! I will always be important to my good friends.

Do parents and blood-related family always come first, or are there times when other relationships are our first consideration? It is quite usual that family relationships take precedence over our everyday friendships. However, there are times when other friendships might take priority over the family. This can be quite difficult to navigate and can place us into conflicts with members of our family. For example, when my partner and I became 'an item' my family were not happy about it. I was a grown-up woman and quite capable of making up my own mind. But this did not impress my family. They believed that I was making the wrong choice and were quite cross with me. Living with the discomfort that this caused was uncomfortable, but I needed to do that. Fortunately, over time, my family adjusted and today are very happy with my choice of partner. But even if they had never come to a place of acceptance of my choice of life partner, my choices in this domain were of greater importance than theirs. I stress, though, that I was in a position to make such a choice because I was over 18 years of age and a mature, capable (in many ways) adult. Now, if I had been immature, under age and not so capable, the situation might have been quite different. My parents would have been right to express their concerns because, as a minor, my decisions might not be fully informed by all the relevant information that comes with more maturity.

Other occasions when you might feel this kind of family conflict occur for a variety of reasons. Maybe the family want you to go on holiday with them, like you have done most years in the past? Maybe they don't think your choice of friends are appropriate? Maybe they think your choice of clothing, hair style, jewellery or body piercing are too influenced by your friends, and they don't approve? The chances are that some or all of these situations might occur for you and your family at some point in time. It seems to me that this is a natural part of growing up, and taking your own place within the world of grown-ups will require you to make decisions that are not always agreed to by one's family. For example, all of us, at one time or another, have chosen our friends over our families!

What do we do if our families don't like our friends? Again this is quite a common scenario…it is something many of us experience at some time or other. The difficulty is, though, that at times our families might be quite discerning and, therefore, judge our 'friends' accurately. What we need to know is: does their judgement have important consequences for us? For example, are these 'friends' relating to us with our best interest at heart, or are they using us for their own devices? If the conclusion is that they are only using us (somewhere to crash, eat, take advantage of our hospitality, borrow our DVDs, CDs, clothes, and so on) then we are better off without them. If, however, our friends genuinely have our interest at heart, but our families don't approve of their fashion sense, jewellery, music tastes, employment status, etc., then we might acknowledge this to them and note their concerns but maintain our friendships. I think the bottom line is that real friends are people who are caring, supportive and loyal in their relationships. If their hair style or fashion sense is not appreciated by all, but their other qualities are, then this is what counts. If this is a dilemma for you and your family, you could try asking your family to list qualities they would value in a friend, then ask them to list the evidence that these qualities are not present in the friends they say they don't approve of.

By the same token though, if this task then demonstrates there are some concerns over our chosen friends, maybe it would be wise to listen to our families. If this task reveals that our family's concerns are groundless, at least we have shown maturity in our handling of this situation and we can show this to our families. This is then a step in the right direction and should earn us their respect.

What do we do if our friends don't like our families? You might have heard the saying 'You can't choose your family but you can choose your friends'. It's fine to have friends who don't appreciate our families…as long as it's for legitimate reasons; for example, the generation gap, nothing in common, and so on. If, however, our friends sense that our families are overprotective, even abusive and too controlling, this is a different matter. Families should be safe havens where we can grow and develop with confidence. Sometimes they are not. I have had encounters with family situations that are not conducive to healthy relationships, and I have even believed it best to encourage one of my friends to distance herself from her family's potential control over her life.

I would hope that this is an exception and that most families understand the changes their offspring need to travel through. Growing up and forming relationships and friendships outside of our family life is necessary for healthy development and eventual separation from parents in order to form our own families.

Sometimes my work means little time for friends; should I try to change this? Well, the question here is 'Are we looking after ourselves?' Being a workaholic might not be good for our health long-term. Usually, time with one's friends is 'down time' or time when we can relax and enjoy some space away from work.

This is time we all need. If our lives are so work-focused that there isn't any time for relaxing, then we might need to re-evaluate our work lifestyle. Of course, there are times when work will dominate and leave us less time for 'play', but this should only be for short spells of time. All very well for me to say this, but my life isn't yours. You are the one who has to decide the balance between work and friends that suits you. Of course, there is time when we are not working but we are not with other friends either. We might need some time for ourselves, time for relaxation pursuits that we enjoy, such as time for pleasure activities, reading, specific hobbies, travel, and so on. Being our own best friend at times is very important!

I'm studying; I've no time for play. Some of us consider study in the same way as we do work. During times of university study I found it much easier to focus upon my studies when I was not interrupted. Other students can manage study and a social life, but I always found this hard. For me it was one or the other; too difficult to do both. I did manage to see friends once my assignments were over, but this was often the time when other students (who might have left their assignments to the last minute) were occupied with their own university work!

I was once told by another student, 'All work and no play makes Jack a dull boy.' For a long time I didn't know what the student meant. I didn't know anyone called Jack! Actually, I now understand this saying. It means that if we spend all of our time working or studying we may become quite boring people and others might not find us interesting. If this is the case, it could become difficult to find friends. Quite often, to find friends, we have to go to places where people meet up for leisure-type activities, such as clubs, pubs and social gatherings. Or, if this is difficult, we might spend the time exploring friendship in other ways, like over the Internet. If, however, we are too occupied with work or study and don't get out and about, or don't make time for friends, we might miss the opportunities to make friends.

So how can I get the right balance between friends, work and family? This requires some attention from us. I find it useful to have an electronic organiser that can be programmed to accommodate work, family and friends. I can use such a device to type in my schedule, making sure I give time for physical exercise, as well as time for the computer. If I schedule physical exercise, like a walk along the sea front or a walk into town, I could also invite a friend to come with me. This way I am taking care of myself and of my friendships. I aim to make sure that meal times are times with the family. If there is a TV programme I'd like to watch and it's showing during a meal time, then I tape it so I can watch it later and it doesn't interrupt my time with the family. When the phone rings I feel urged to answer it. It doesn't matter what time of day it is. So, during meal times or important family times, I let the answer machine get the telephone messages and I can listen to them later at a more convenient time. This way I don't miss a call from my friends, but I take care of myself and my family too.

Hi Ho

Hi ho, hi ho, it's off to work we go.
We work all day and get no play,
But at the end of every day,
We have the joy of earning our pay.

Hi ho, hi ho, it's to the bills we go.
I earn to spend and pay my way,
So we can live another day,
I only reap when I can sow.

Hi ho, hi ho, knee deep in debt I go.
We need new things,
Our mindset sings,
A car, a lounge suite, all for show.

Hi ho, hi ho, it's to my grave I go.
I lived real well, materially,
My friends had theirs too, fashionably.
But the thing I noticed before I died,
Was that all of those things stayed well behind.

If only I had spent more time,
On earning less and gaining more,
The treasure money just can't buy,
The love of one's friends as time passes by.
Hi ho, hi ho, it's to the dust we go.

Getting the balance right between work, family and friends can be a delicate issue. When I'm focused I don't like to be interrupted. Usually this is because the smallest interruption disturbs my ability to know where I've been and where I'm going. So, if interrupted, I often lose my place in a situation and might even need to start over again from the beginning.

This means that I can get really frustrated and irritated by interruptions! Unfortunately though, my friends might not know this. You see, lots of people seem able to refocus upon what they were doing after an interruption, and it doesn't seem to phase them. If they are upset about it, they might know this in advance and can say, 'Please don't interrupt me, I need to focus.' This is a useful skill, but not one I'm very good at! If you think you fit this profile, you might want to warn your friends so that they know in advance not to interrupt you, or, at least, to give you some advance warning of pending circumstances.

It is also helpful to make a 'time' to catch up with one's friends rather than just have them turn up to visit you or you to visit them. You can then do your best to reduce interruptions by putting the phone on to answer machine, and so on. Another advantage of planned time is that you will know how long the time together might last, i.e. start and finish times.

Many of my friends take their time saying goodbye. I might expect them to leave at an agreed time: 'I'll be over about seven o'clock this evening,' says Janet, 'and stay for a couple of hours.' This lets me know that Janet should arrive at approximately 7pm give or take 5–10 minutes, and she will leave again at approximately 9pm give or take 5–10 minutes. However, what tends to happen is that Janet's leaving period of time can take a bit longer than her arrival period. She might start to say things like 'Well, I should be going then', which is more an announcement of her intention to leave rather than that of an abrupt departure. Her actual leaving might take another 15 minutes.

What about the inevitable? The inevitable is an expression people use to describe an event which they think of as 'this was bound to happen' or 'there is no way out of this'. The inevitable might occur anywhere, at any time and with anyone. If we know that these things happen, then we can prepare a little for it. When someone says 'it's inevitable', we know it might not have anything to do with us…it 'was bound to happen', and so on. If this is the case, we do not need to feel guilty or responsible for it; it's just one of those things. However, the inevitable might also come with attachments. For example, if you play with fire it's inevitable that you will get burnt.

I found this understanding helpful because, even though I often do feel responsible, I can tell my feelings that they are ill informed. You see, sometimes our feelings are not associated with the reality of the situation so much as they might be connected to what we think is the reality. This means that if *I think* I am responsible my emotions will agree (*I feel*), even when my thinking is wrong. Therefore I often check in on my thinking (take a reality check) so I can challenge my feelings. It doesn't mean my feelings change immediately, but as I change my thinking it filters through to my feelings and allows my emotive state to adapt accordingly. For example: My friend comes to visit and later she leaves. Then the phone rings. It is my friend who tells me she has left her bag behind at my place. 'Oh, I'm sorry,' I say. 'It's not your fault,' my friend replies. 'I'm the one who forgot it.' I don't know why I so often feel responsible for stuff that isn't mine, but belongs to other people. I'm learning to deal with this but it does take time.

Oh well! The inevitable also applies to things like public transport running late, being 'stuck' in traffic, getting sick, losing things, upsetting some people, computer crashes, raining on your nearly dry washing, shopping bags breaking, shoe laces snapping, misplacing your keys, over-keeping a library book or DVD, spilling your coffee, disagreeing with friends, and so on (to name a few). If we accept that these things happen, we can learn the 'Oh well!' expression and dismiss them. Of course, if it's related to our friendships, then we need to amend our discrepancies (agree to disagree perhaps) and get on with things. Life is too short to waste it on feeling cross with friends. Then again, quite often our feeling angry or upset only hurts us, no one else, so it's not good for our health either!

Coping with chaos. I have some friends whose abilities to maintain order in their daily lives can be quite difficult. I come from a family where order in the home (e.g. tidy home, cleanliness, things in their proper places, etc.) was seen as a matter of importance. I myself have always had some difficulty with this. I'm quite capable of maintaining orderliness in my home as long as I've nothing else to do and the home is orderly to start with! As soon as chaos starts to build up around me, especially in the form of paperwork, I can feel totally overwhelmed. I might organise my mess into neat piles and create space to sit, eat or work, but that's usually as ordered as I can get it. Actually clearing those piles away and dealing with the paperwork is a horrendous job for me, and so one I avoid.

As most of you know, order and structure are paramount for us, as individuals on the autistic spectrum. I function best when my life is planned, structured and prepared for. This includes the physical environment that I live and operate in. There are days when I can't think because of the chaos around me. It's so hard trying to maintain order and understanding within my thinking processes that if chaos exists around me then my ability to process, understand and connect to others is inhibited. I experience shopping centres, places full of people and happenings, towns, concerts, public transport, etc. as very chaotic and, therefore, very difficult to cope with. How friends can chat to one another and enjoy each other's company in such places is very difficult for me to understand. It's like trying to have a conversation amongst a jungle of screaming children!

Unfortunately, some of my friends' homes can also be like this. Instead of an ordered structure where everything is in its place, enabling relaxed attention to conversation, some homes I visit are chaotic masterpieces of noise, messiness and disorganisation, and a frightening kaleidoscope of difficulty! I love my friends, but some of their family homes can add a dimension of difficulty that I find hard to cope with. *How do you say to a friend 'Yes, I'd love to come over as long as the children are not there?'* I can cope with being surrounded by a messy environment, as long as the relevant spaces for sitting, etc. are clear, but noisy children, argumentative individuals, unclear directions and broken promises are very difficult to cope with. I am likely to avoid going to homes that are like this. So instead I try to arrange to meet my friends on common or familiar ground that suits us both, where someone else has ordered things for us and we can just enjoy being together. This might be a quiet café or park near home, it might mean going for a ride into the countryside, where we can walk and talk together quietly. My good friends would not take offence at this, they would understand.

I'm just not good at doing 'friends'. The extract concerning friendship below is uncomfortable to read, but many of you will identify with it. How many of us have wanted to have and be friends, but have felt unsuccessful? How many of us feel unimportant and are convinced other people we like won't like us? Maybe we have some work to do on our belief and schema systems? Maybe we need courage to challenge these? Maybe we need other people to hang in with us on this journey so we don't need to feel quite so alone? Are we ready?

Liam: I'm an Aspie, and that means I'm very monotropic.

Wendy: So, what does that mean for friendship?

Liam: Well…it means that I tend to expect a lot from my friends. I'm an 'all or nothing' type of person. I might attach obsessively to a friend or keep my distance. So, at times I think it's better not to have the complication of having friends. In fact I actually feel that most people don't like me and don't find me very interesting at all. I have often thought that I don't really have friends.

Wendy: I wonder what your concept of 'friend' is? We each need different people in our lives for different reasons, so some friends we might see often and others hardly at all. But both are friends to us in their own way.

Liam: Well…I usually only have friends via other people and I often feel like an idiot when in their company.

Wendy: I don't think others think of you as an idiot though.

Liam: Words are not easy for me, Wendy, I find it hard to keep up with a conversation and follow what's happening. I don't feel very intelligent and I often feel intimidated during academic conversations. In social get-togethers I'm quite lost. It's only one-to-one that I feel any degree of confidence and that changes from person to person.

Wendy: But that's OK. Lots of us feel that way. Friends, who know us, accept us for who we are. I think most of us feel inadequate at times and very few people actually feel as confident as they seem.

Liam: Well...I still don't feel comfortable around people. I think the idea of friends is very good and I would like to have friends. I just think I don't do 'friends' very well.

Wendy: Do you think of your family as 'friends'?

Liam: Yes, in some ways. They are family and I'm used to them. I don't think they know me very well, but I am comfortable around them. Family is family and friends are friends. They are separate institutions with separate expectations. It's easier to be with family because they are family and it's what we are used to.

Being a friend to an individual like Liam is not an easy proposition. We need to look past his difficulties and see the positive things he could bring into any friendship. Helping Liam to see these himself is the ultimate goal. As we hang in with our friends we can be positive role models to each other. When we each experience the negative aspects of who we are, we can assert: 'Yep, that's part of who we are, but there is so much more to discover.' Now, we can take a horse to water but we can't make it drink. This is a saying that means 'we can show someone what they need to do (think, be) but we can't make them take that understanding on board'. We each have a free will of our own. So, it's up to each of us to choose. Taking a risk is part of the friendship journey.

CHAPTER 6

Sharing Common Goals

 **Sharing common goals means that we have similar aims in life.** One of the things about friendship is that even though it might seem difficult forming a friendship in the first place, it might take even more work to maintain it. Having things in common and working together to accomplish shared goals is part of the recipe for successful friendships.

Shared goals can be anything from doing the shopping together to running some type of group activity. When we 'pull' together we walk the same way. There are many ways to share together, and some are more intimate than others. With some of our friends we might feel confident sharing our toothbrush, but with other friends a car ride or a picnic might be as intimate as we can comfortably get!

I have read that in order to have friends one needs to show oneself to be friendly. What does this mean? Being friendly doesn't always mean being the same to everyone. Being friendly to the bus driver really means more like being polite and respectful. However, being friendly to the new kid in class or the new person at our workplace means a bit more than just being polite and respectful, it requires more of our time and attention. It might mean we shadow them for a while until they know their way around better. We might introduce them to some of our friends so they know some people to hang out with, and so on. Eventually they will establish themselves and will not need us so much. They may continue to be friendly with us, but might prefer to hang out with others. This is all part of finding our way and our place in the world around us.

When I moved house I eventually introduced myself to my neighbours. Just because we live next door to one another does not mean that we will become best friends, but I want my neighbours to know that I am friendly and approachable. Sometimes we talk to one another across the garden fence. Sometimes we share a meal or a walk together. Sometimes we go for weeks without seeing one another. We try to look out for one another and are mindful of each other's homes when the other is away. This is called 'being a good neighbour'.

Should I call on all of the neighbours in my street and take them home-made cookies? Well this depends upon you and the neighbours in your street. I live in quite a long street and would have too many neighbours to call on or bake for. The only neighbours I really can accommodate, time-wise, are those closest to me. So I would not bake for all of my neighbours, but I might bake for those closest to my home, i.e. next door and across from me.

What about the television concept of 'friends'? There is a TV programme called *Friends* and there are several 'soaps' or TV shows that suggest friends are all of the individuals in our apartment block or street. This is not always the case. It is possible to live somewhere and not have any of your friends live near you. This is especially true in our busy cities where we may never meet our neighbours. Television programmes are often dramatised, and this means that, although there are elements of 'real life' associations within the scripted performances, they may not be reflective of our real lives.

What if my neighbours don't want to be friendly? Each individual has the right to choose how friendly or unfriendly they want to be. It's not always possible or desirable for us to know what might be happening in the life of our neighbours. Sometimes things happen to or for people that are upsetting or difficult to cope with. These life events can happen to us and to our neighbours. Of course, this may have nothing to do with us, but it might mean they don't 'feel' like being very friendly to other people. This may mean they can seem unfriendly to us. If this happens to us, it might be a good idea to respond with politeness and respect but aim to give our neighbours some space and try not to take their apparent lack of friendliness personally.

On the other hand, we may have neighbours who are polite but not available to us as friends. This can happen for a variety of reasons. They may be too busy with family and work to have time for 'extra' friends. They may live a different lifestyle from us, and this could mean we have little in common. Without common goals and interests, there isn't the cement that binds people together. Friends need to have common goals and interests to share together. Do you know the feeling of meeting someone who is likeminded? Isn't this just the best thing! You just 'click' together and recognise that you have a kindred spirit. True friendship and real bonds of friendship tend to be forged when people have lots in common.

At times our common goals are short-term (we are on the same committee, we met at a college enrolment day, our kids went to school together); at other times those common interests and goals can last a lifetime (we grew up together, we were in the same band, we share the same interest in animals, and so on).

Should I leave some people to be on their own or should I always try to jolly them along and keep bothering them until they give in? I have some friends who say things like 'Cheer up'; 'Smile'; 'Oh come on, it will be good for you.' These friends are often well-meaning, but I don't always want to be cheered up and might just want to be left on my own to deal with what's happening for me. You might feel like this at times too. So, yes, there are times when we can encourage our friends to 'cheer up', but there are also times when we need to give our friends some space and let them be. When I am unsure of the best thing to do for my friends, who might be in this situation, I can check it out with them by saying: 'Is there a possibility I can cheer you up or do you want me to leave you alone for a while?'

I do want to have friends but I prefer it if they joined in with me and with my interests. Is this selfish? Should I try to find friends who share an interest with me, or should I try to accommodate the things that interest them but don't interest me? This is often a difficult task for all of us, but I think it's extra hard for those of us with autism and Asperger's syndrome. Due to the way my head functions I tend to need to be single-minded and focused in order to accommodate and attend to words or actions going on around and within me. I'm not good at doing more than one thing at any one time, unless it's already accommodated within my interest system. So this will mean it's difficult for me to attend to something outside of my interest system. For example, my friend says, 'Oh look at that dress. I like that. What do you think?' My response might disappoint my friend because my attention will not be on the dress and I won't have any 'thoughts' about it. Therefore, I am likely to say, 'What dress?... Oh, that dress... I don't know. It's a dress.' My friend wants me to imagine the dress on her. She wants my opinion about its suitability for her. Will it look good on her? Should she consider buying it? In all honesty I am unlikely to know. I am not interested in dresses and I'm not good at imagining what they might look like on someone.

However, if my friend had said, 'Oh, look at that cat. Isn't she gorgeous?', my interest would be aroused immediately. I love cats and can easily relate to their loveliness! 'But, isn't this rude?' you might ask. 'I mean, we can't always share a common interest, but we need to learn how to show interest in things we don't find interesting, especially if they are interesting to our friends.' I have some thoughts about this.

I used to think that if I wasn't interested then I'm not interested! My lack of interest, or my expectation that my friend should know I'm not interested, caused some problems for me with my friendships. Now I understand how I can show interest even when I'm not interested. This is not so much a lie as it is a desirable decision for action. For example, you might have experienced times when you just have to comply to an instruction, even though you really don't want to. Your complying is the right response (cross the road appropriately, say hello to someone, let the dentist look at your teeth, have that needle, complete that assignment, and so on) but you would rather have done something else! This decision to attend to an area that doesn't interest you but is either for your 'good' or 'the common good' is kind of like choosing to show interest when you are not interested.

We are doing this for the good of our friendship. It requires our time and some phrases to accompany that time. So I learnt to say 'Yes, that's nice' or 'I'm glad you like that' in response to someone saying that they liked something. If their comment was one of dislike or disapproval, then I learnt to say something like 'Oh…how difficult for you' or 'Yes, that's uncomfortable for you'. These phrases let the person know you heard them and are interested in the things they think and feel. It does not necessarily mean that you always agree with them.

Choosing the moment. 'A Friend is someone who understands your past, believes in your future and accepts you today the way you are.' I have these words on a fridge magnet and they often remind me of our human disposition. I want my friends to accept who I am but I need to accept who they are too. If you like the idea of sharing some of your time and life with friends then you will need to learn how to pick your moments. By this I mean learning the lesson of what to share, when and with whom.

When we share a common goal or purpose with another person, it is likely that they will see us in many of our different moods and moments. However, maintaining our dignity and respecting theirs isn't always easy. I remember one friend saying, 'I don't want you to see me like this.' My first thought was 'But this is who you are today', and I couldn't understand their concerns. I was tempted to say 'Why not? This is part of who you are' and just ignore their words. That would not have been a good idea though. I have learnt that to some people outward appearances are very important and they need to 'present well outwardly' to feel inwardly OK about themselves. If I had ignored their words they might also have felt I had ignored their feelings, and this could impact negatively upon their ability to trust me with their real selves in the future.

There are times in my life when I am prone to 'autistic meltdown'. These times are both terrifying and exhausting. I wouldn't wish them upon anyone. Unless you experience this it is highly unlikely that you can imagine what this feels like. Unfortunately, I can't choose these moments and I can't choose when to have them or who to be around at the time. These times are when I cannot cope with a situation and I have run out of resources or energy that would usually enable me to respond differently. For example: I was in town accompanying a friend whilst she did her shopping. The friend said she wanted to go into a particular shop. 'No problem,' I said as I went into the shop with her. Once inside this quite large, busy and chaotic shop, there was loud, upbeat music playing. There were also lots and lots of fluorescent lights, crowds of people, children and a screaming baby! I might have managed one of these events but definitely not all of them. I said to my friend, as I pointed in the direction of what I thought was a general exit, 'I'll wait outside for you.' She nodded and was making her way to the check-out with her purchase as I began to leave the shop. Once outside I waited for my friend. Five, ten, fifteen minutes went by. My friend did not appear from the shop. I began to feel a sense of panic. Going back into the shop was something I wanted to avoid, but I wondered why she had not come out. Eventually I went back inside and walked around the whole shop looking for her, but I could not find her. By now I was really panicking. I could not remember where the car was or even where I was! I began to hum out loud, cover my ears with my hands, rock and walk about in an erratic manner and cry all at the same time. I called her name and raced about, but she was not there.

Eventually, I went back outside the shop and paced up and down in front of it. From all outward appearances I looked like a deranged, middle-aged, overweight, poorly dressed moron! People gave me a wide berth. I was in this state for almost an hour. Then, one moment, as I looked across the road from the shop corner and I thought I saw a green padded shirt making a phone call from the public phone box, in my pocket my mobile phone shrieked and vibrated; it was my friend!

Although we had found one another I was emotionally and physically exhausted. At first I could not speak and I allowed her to lead me to the car where I could simply sit and have nothing more required of me. On this occasion I had been found and nothing too untoward had happened. In the past I'd had occasions when I had been arrested, locked up and treated as if I were a threat to myself and to others. All that had really happened was I had lost my way and, like a small child, my lost state caused me to panic. These moments in time occur less frequently than when I was a child, but they still happen. Do you want to be a friend to someone who experiences these times? How would you cope? What could we organise to help us get through such times? What if I cannot choose my moments?

It would be a good idea if I could explain these times to my friends and prepare them in advance. My difficulty is, though, that I don't know when they will happen nor what to do to avoid them. Oh well, I can take some precautions of course. I can try to avoid busy, noisy places. I can try to avoid noisy, busy people. I can try to avoid over-demand upon my time and energy. I can try to avoid life! Unfortunately, being autistic predisposes me to these types of difficulty; it comes with the territory. My friends might need to understand this, and, just as they would have me accept them for who they are, I need acceptance too.

Moments

> I wander around inside of this space trying to
>   recognise anyone's face.
> These people and places just fill up the spaces and all
>   merge into boxes and cases.
> There's boxes of books and people with looks, all
>   seem like strangers in very dark suits.
> What is this place? Where is my space? What is my
>   name? What is this game?
> If I knew the rules, would it help me to find all of
>   those things that got left behind?
> If I found my way, would it be better today, or would
>   it just leave me alone the next way?
> I don't seem able to master the knack; the knack that
>   lets me find my way back.
> Even when I get it right at the time, I lose it again on
>   the very next line.
> Will you still travel this way with me? Will you take
>   my hand and help me to stand?

I know it's not easy, being my friend, but I'd like you
    with me, in spite of this trend.
I've other qualities and other times. I'm not just a
    bundle of broken up chimes.
Come explore this life with me. We will have adven-
    tures, I can guarantee!

What's common and normal for me might not be for you.
We each can become so used to the way we do things that we fail
to recognise that not everyone does things the way we do them. I
have friends who drink their tea black, would not wear jeans, only
go out in public if they have makeup on and don't wear pyjamas in
bed! These things are quite strange to me and I find the way they
live and do things quite difficult to comprehend.

The good news is that in order to share common interests and
goals we do not have to be and do things the same way. In fact,
being different adds a sense of mystery and intrigue to most relationships, and this can be a good thing. If we were all the same in
every area of our lives, we would be boring and there wouldn't be
anything to discover about each other. The other bit of good news
is that I don't have to understand why you are different to me
(phew), I just need to accept that you are!

So, having things in common with our friends and sharing
common goals is good and will help to develop our friendships.
Being different people with different likes, wants, needs and
desires is also healthy and, as long as our values are similar, will be
good for our friendships.

What about belief systems? I said in the Introduction that each
of us has a personal belief system that might be responsible for
sabotaging our friendships. I now want to explore this further and
offer some hope for those of us who fit this description.

At times my life has been a conflict between what I would like
to have happen and what I believe will happen. For example, I

would like my friends to know me and accept me for who I am. I have no problem accepting them. But what tends to happen is that I believe if they really knew me they would not accept me! Maybe you can identify with this. In the past I have had other similar beliefs. For example, the belief that I am not intelligent; the belief that when people see the real Wendy they will realise that she isn't able to be who they need and, therefore, they will disown her; the belief that all good things will end, so friends will always leave me; and the belief that I will never be 'good' enough to have friends of any value.

Belief systems are strong medicine! Quite often what I believe will happen to me, really does. For example, if I expect that I will get lost (as usual), then I often do. If I expect that things won't go well, this expectation often comes true. Now we could say to ourselves 'Yep, this is just what I thought would happen' and as we do so we keep our belief systems fuelled and fired up ready to repeat and perpetuate our beliefs day after day. Or we can aim to acquire the courage necessary to process this whole scenario and explore ways to change our belief systems.

What has this to do with friendship? Everything! You see, if I continually work hard to maintain a belief system that says I am unworthy of friends; I don't need other people; my Asperger's or autism will stop me having friends; friends always leave me in the end; and other such beliefs, then we are the ones who are maintaining a mindset that will bring the above about. We might not have been the person to start this belief system, but we will be contributing to it.

Have you ever met anyone who has said to you 'I'm not good at relationships', or maybe you know someone who always seems to pick the wrong people to be their friends? I've done this time and time again. What I have come to understand is, although not conscious of it, I have chosen the wrong people to relate to.

In the past these have been individuals who have lots of needs of their own that they have expected Wendy to meet. Wendy inevitably fails to meet those needs, and Wendy's beliefs are confirmed ('I'm not good at friendship; people will discover what I'm like and leave me').

Why do I choose such 'needy' individuals? Well, maybe initially we appear to have lots in common. Maybe in some ways they were like me and it seemed we were part of the same journey. Maybe we seemed to have common goals. I'm not saying that we shouldn't be friendly to others who have deep needs or that we should move away from our friends at such times. But if the friends we appear to be relating to have poor autonomy, and we have the belief system that perpetuates broken friendships, then we might be setting our friendships up for failure without a lot of effort!

What I have discovered is that there is a remedy for this. I work hard these days on my own self-confidence issues. These are issues that were propagated within my life right from early childhood. What does the deficit model of disability inspire within us? Does it inspire confidence and healthy self-esteem? No, it inspires deficits! Like so many of us, I grew up believing that I was a dud, a person of little value to society because of my inability to learn at the same rate as others or because of my difficulties with social expectation. Difficulty is not the same thing as deficit. How does one become the other? It seems to me to be a societal failure and one we all contribute to, however unwittingly. The good news is that we are the ones who can change this.

What if one of our goals was to build our own self-confidence and personal autonomy? That would be a great place to start to lay down a good foundation for successful friendships. Recently I visited a friend and shared with her my story of failure to feel 'valued' in one of my relationships. She said to me, 'Wendy, I have something here that will help you.' She went to one of the rooms in her house and came back with a particular object. She took my hand gently and placed the object in my palm and folded my fingers over it. She said, 'Whenever you are in a situation with this friend and their words are causing you discomfort, I want you to take this object into your hands. As you feel this object ask yourself the question "What does Wendy want?"' You see, that friend knew that I needed some type of prompt that would enable me to make time for the processing of my thinking and checking in on my own thoughts, desires, wishes and needs. This could then facilitate my responses to others and allow me the value of my personhood, rather than being a person who agreed with actions by saying 'yes' to them but feeling 'uncomfortable' about it and not knowing why.

I found that my being assertive caused a ripple effect amongst my friends. Some of that rippling was uncomfortable, mostly because my friends were not used to Wendy being assertive. This discomfort wasn't nice, but it was important to weather it and get beyond it. By 'sticking to my guns' and not opting out if friends reacted negatively to me, I won their respect and became a more desirable person to have as a friend. I'm sharing this with you because it works and it's so much nicer than failing at friendship all the time.

I might not be able to go back and fix those friendships that ended for one reason or another, but I choose my friends wisely now, am not co-dependent, and my expectation is that my friendships will prosper not expire! This can be true for you too. Why not give it a shot? What do you have to lose? You might change a belief system that has served you well in achieving negative outcomes, where relationships are concerned, and it's a rut that is soul-destroying. The thing is it's also a rut we know well, which takes courage to climb out of. You don't have to do this on your own. There are organisations that can support you. Maybe you could check it out? There is a short list of organisations that work with mediation and relationships at the end of this book (Appendix 2). Why maintain the status quo when we don't have to?

CHAPTER 7

Baring All

I think one should be free to be oneself in the company of one's friends, but is there a limit to this? If there is a limit, how will I know what it is? Yes, one should be free to be oneself with one's friends, but we need to check that this is done with respect for our friends, and for oneself. Respecting oneself will mean that I care for myself and my friendships like I might tend to a beautiful garden to keep it looking at its best.

This might mean a bit of work, but it is less work if I care constantly than if I let it go and allow the weeds to take over. Recently I recognised that I wasn't caring for my life as much as I should be, and this was influencing my friendships negatively. Because I wasn't tending to myself very well and was feeling depressed about some things, I began to let care of myself slip. This attitude flowed out into areas of my health and my friends noticed that I was having a hard time. When spoken to about it I shrugged it off and kept going. This then meant that my friendships were being burdened by my lack of care, and this began to show on them. Eventually Wendy was back on the merry-go-round of self-pity and despair – not a pretty sight! How do you feel when you are with individuals who are feeling sorry for themselves? I expect you feel uncomfortable and start avoiding them. Yep, that old abandonment schema tries very hard to get back into our lives…well, guess what, it doesn't have to succeed! If we have the courage to be ourselves with our friends, then it means owning who we are and allowing them to speak into our lives. I need to listen to my friends, weigh up their advice and then choose a course of action. I'm working on this carefully because I don't want to choose a course of action that is unrealistic and will only lead to my failing again.

Let me explain. If we set goals for ourselves that are too high, we will only be adding to our negative belief systems about ourselves because we are bound to fail. For example, I am overweight and I want to address this by changing my lifestyle. But, radical lifestyle change will probably not work for me in my situation, so it is doomed from the start. I will then think, 'See, I can't get anything right. I'm just no good at anything.' My next step, in line with my destructive belief system, is to give up trying and move back into depression, which will fuel my belief and maintain it. So, the better option is to make small changes to my lifestyle that can become routine and have a better chance of succeeding. These small changes, for Wendy, might be putting less butter on her bread (not, no butter at all), getting a bit more exercise (use the stairs, not the lift; walk where possible rather than use the car), eat regularly, but on a smaller plate so it's easier to have smaller helpings, and aim to deal effectively with stress (I'm not too good at this) and accept my limitations.

How I think about myself will influence my friendships. This might be part of the reason we tidy our home and clean the bathroom before we have guests. We want our friends and family to feel comfortable in our home and in our company. If we are feeling good about ourselves, this helps others to feel good too.

'Yes, but I think my friends should accept me the way I am. If my home is a mess, or I am, they shouldn't mind.' Quite right, but taking care of our home and ourselves isn't the same thing as having our friends accept us the way we are. Even when friends accept us the way we are (which might mean being in a state of messiness, chaos and disorder) and that includes our home, they might feel more comfortable if we and our home showed care. I want my friends to know that I accept them too and, for some of them, a clean bathroom and a space to sit with me (amongst my chaos) will help them feel at ease. My friends know that organising myself, my home (includes housework) and my life is not my forte! I'm not good at it, so my home will be a reflection of this. They love and accept me the way I am. But, it doesn't take much to make sure my untidy spaces include a clean bathroom and relative cleanliness in the kitchen (whatever relative means).

Baring all and having my friends see me as I am is a mutual state, that means it works both ways. This is good, but I still need to care for me and my friendships in order to keep them safe.

Public and private tend to be terms that I associate with someone's property. If the sign says 'Private' then I know not to go there without permission. If the sign says 'Public' (as in public footpath or public house) then I know I have right of way or right of access. These terms can also apply to areas of one's life and person. For example, people need privacy for aspects of their lives that are not for public access. This might apply to their mail, their home, their mobile phone, their personal belongings, their handbags, their coat and pants pockets, their email, their personal thoughts, secrets and body. If my friend gives me permission to open their mail or go into their bedroom, even though it's usually their private area, I will be allowed on occasion. It's important to my friendships that I don't take these things for granted though, and that I check in often with my friends. Just as we would expect our friends to respect us and our things, so we need to respect them and their things. Just because they have given us permission for one occasion, it doesn't automatically entitle us to permanent access any time we feel like it.

I'm mentioning this because in the past I have overstepped the mark with my friends in this area. One of my friends shared some personal things with me and I failed to recognise that this was for that time only. I assumed that, having that one experience, meant I could be part of their lives in that way at any time. I've also noted that some of my friends have assumed the same with me. Once when I was ill and in bed a male friend came over to visit me. Since that occasion this same friend has thought it OK to come into my bedroom at any time. I need to be able to say to him gently, 'Please don't come into my room unless I invite you. This applies to all times.' It's not that we don't value our friends and want them to share in our lives, but there are times when we value our privacy too and this is important to us. If we are unsure of what might be private for our friends or if we feel we need to tell them what is private for us, then we can talk it over with them and this keeps things clear between us.

Revealing or rude. Learning how to trust one's instincts and be in tune with one's friends isn't easy for anyone. But, for some of us, it can be even harder. For example, I can be so focused upon something of interest to me that I fail to note my surroundings or the mood of my friends. I remember one occasion when I needed the bathroom. We had been out on an excursion and I had failed to recognise the urgency of my need. Then, just as we sat down in a restaurant for a meal, I became acutely aware that my bladder was about to burst. As I rose from the table and headed towards the restrooms, I started to undo the zipper on my pants. My friend, who had jumped up from the table when I did and was walking with me to make sure I found the way, said, 'No, Wendy, wait until you are inside the cubicle with the door shut before you unzip your pants.' Usually I am very aware of what is public and what is private, but there are occasions when I forget!

There are rules which can help us to know what the expectation or limit is on physical behaviour, speech, dress code and various interventions. These rules may change according to the situation we are in and the people we are with. It's a good idea to become familiar with these rules. This can be difficult when the rules are only 'understood' to be in operation and are not actually written down or spelled out to us. The basic rules, however, are based upon the ideas of mutual respect and understanding. For example: I will aim to value you and respect your person, personal belongings and personhood. I will try to treat you with the same esteem as I would want you to treat me.

Some friends enjoy a hug and a kiss on the cheek, others do not. So, when we first meet up with our friends, we can extend a handshake in their direction and leave it at that. Usually shaking hands with someone is an acceptable greeting that meets with the approval of most other people, so we can feel pretty safe in greeting someone in this manner.

Then there are times when a friend might move towards us and want to hug or squeeze us in some way. It's OK to extend one's hand to intercept this if one isn't comfortable with such close physical contact. It's also OK to accept the hug and leave it at that. It might simply be a greeting, like the handshake, and not be anything more.

What if I really like the feeling of physical contact, should I hug them more often and hold them close to me each time we meet? What are the rules here? The rules are that we don't do anything that the other person is uncomfortable with. Even if we like it, they might not. So we need to check in with them and ask them how they feel about this. I give my friends permission to let me know what their boundaries are because I recognise that I might not be good at reading them myself. Sometimes we might have very strong feelings for someone, either good feelings or uncomfortable feelings. But just because we have these feelings, it doesn't mean these feelings are allowed to be expressed physically. First we need to ask ourselves some questions so we can check our feelings out and assess potential outcomes for us and our friendships. We need to do this when we are away from the individual we are feeling this about, and we can have the time and the space to process what we feel.

Some questions we might ask ourselves:

- *Is what I feel the usual feeling that can be expressed publicly or is this usually a private feeling?* For example, some forms of kissing, hugging and passionate embrace might not be so much a public activity as it is personal. So, we need to check that this is what the other person wants too and whether or not they feel comfortable engaging with us in public. If they are not comfortable in public but are comfortable in private, then we can both enjoy this privately together. Anger and disapproval can be strong emotions too. There are times we might feel very upset and want to hit out at someone or something. Usually this type of feeling is not to be expressed publicly. There may be some exceptions to this though; for example, injustice makes me angry and I'm not good at being quiet about it. However, if I thump someone, I might only hurt them physically and this might not help! So, I try to harness my anger and use it constructively to address the situation.

Maybe I can write a letter or arrange to talk about it. This
is more likely to enable my feelings to get a hearing than if
I am physically abusive causing those involved to switch
off from me.

- *Kiss on the cheek or on the lips?* Usually a cheek is right for
  friends or family, and lips work for lovers, partners or
  spouses.

- *Is what I feel shared by my friend and are they happy for us to
  physically express our affection or anger in this manner?* If they
  are not comfortable, then we should avoid the physical
  expression of these emotions and explore alternatives, e.g.
  written expression. However, if even the written form of
  communication is rejected by our friends, we may need to
  leave it there. I know this is hard, it's happened to me, but
  if we pursue someone who does not want to be pursued by
  us, we place our own lives and health at risk. It's better to
  let those friends be and focus upon our other friends or on
  developing new friendships.

So, once we have assessed our feelings, physically and emotionally, and have checked in with our friends as to what they are comfortable with, we can begin to learn and understand the needs of
our individual friendships. Then, we each can feel safe in exploring our friendships.

**What if we have to do something else and we can't see our
friends for a while?** This is a common scenario for many of us.
Usually friends understand when we are busy because they have
these times too.

So, what if we have huge chunks of time between us and lots
of kilometres? How do we maintain our friendships when we are
apart? The good news is that there is email, the telephone, letter
exchange and occasional visits. Most friends accept that this is
part of life and it happens to most of us.

What if we find ourselves in new situations and need to make new friends? Will there be space in people's lives for us, or will they have enough friends already and won't want any more friends? For most of us, discovering new friendships and new people to be friends with is all part of the friendship adventure. It's about 'back-up', you see. We all need back-up. This is an expression that means we need extras – extra friends to be a friend with when other friends are busy. Extra supportive individuals may seem superfluous to one's needs at times, but you never know when we each might need the other. Safety in numbers has a nice ring to it!

Can I count upon my friends? How will I know if they are telling me things they think I want to hear rather than things I need to hear? Some might argue that these sentiments are actually the same. But, I have noted that there are times when people seem to appreciate what their friends want to hear but know the difference between fulfilling that desire legitimately and telling them what they need to hear! If I only hear the words that make me feel good (even if they are true), then I will build up a false picture of reality and I will be living a lie. I would rather that my friends be honest with me, even if I don't like it. We can let our friends know that this is our wish. Then, at least because we have shared our views with our friends, it's more likely that they will honour this and aim to be honest with us.

Is there a limit to what a friendship can go through? One would be tempted to think that friendship might mean 'no limits' to what one could go through. Actually I think there are more limits on friendship than there are on lots of other things. Some limits are set because of the nature of the relationship. Intimate friendships of a sexual or romantic nature may include sexual intimacy; this isn't usual with a non-romantic or platonic friendship. Platonic friendships 'bare all' in a different way. They may bare their soul to one another, but not their bodies. For example, if you were a very close friend of mine, I might tell you about things I think and feel. We might go out together to places of mutual interest and share food, music, activities and conversation, but we probably wouldn't share in lots of physical contact such as kissing, cuddling and sexual intercourse. These types of encounters are reserved for romantic and sexual relationships between consenting adults.

Other limits might be based on things like personality, gender, interests, availability of time, age, health and one's other commitments. What type of person are you? What type of personality is your friend? You see, if you are the type of person who loves being outside in all weathers and could walk for hours across rugged countryside, but your friend is more of a stay-at-home person who isn't too keen on getting their feet wet or shoes dirty, then your times together roaming the countryside might be limited. To accommodate each other's interests you might share in activities you both enjoy, but these will probably be limited because you are different types of people.

At times one is limited quite naturally by one's gender. It's not so much 'anything you can do I can do better', but if I am female my physical strength might not be my forte (unless I'm a body builder or health junkie), so I might not really enjoy hours on end of lifting weights or other such physical demands. Some would say that being female means we are the stronger sex. For example, female-coded sperm seems to be larger and stronger than male sperm. Females live longer than males, generally speaking, and females are often tougher than males when it comes to handling pain. But female energy often goes to our emotive and orchestrating roles, rather than to physical muscle development. So, within the roles that demand physical strength, we might well discover our limitations when relating to male friends. I have usually won arm-wrestling competitions with other female friends, but rarely have I won against the guys!

One's interests usually place another natural limitation upon friendships. For example, I love watching science fiction, but many of my friends do not. This means they might come to watch a science-fiction movie with me, but they won't come often. I love birds and animals and enjoy visiting bird and animal parks and zoos. My friends might enjoy these too, but, again, will only want to do this on occasion; whereas I would get the season ticket and visit as often as I could! Although we may have lots of interests in common with our friends, and frequently share the same likes and dislikes, we might still find limitations due to the differences between us in the depth and extent of our interests.

Time, for many of us, poses definite limitations upon our friendships. I would love to do so much more with my friends, but I don't have the time. My time goes upon so many different things, e.g. work-related topics, study and research, family and household commitments and time out for me. Part of being a good friend to oneself is taking the time to look after oneself. It's only too easy to put everyone else first and not take time for oneself.

I remember when I was first married how I made sure my husband was taken care of. I gave him the best piece of meat, made sure his clothes were dry, that our home was tidy for him to come home to, and so on. When the children were born I focused upon their needs. Wendy's needs always came last. Now this is maybe how it should be, but if we are not careful we neglect ourselves and don't legitimately care for ourselves. This isn't good, because we risk being doormats for others and, perhaps, being boring too!

Whose Time Is This?

It's 7am and the alarm clock beckons,
'Time to wake up' my little clock reckons.
'Oh just a few minutes more,
Then I'll get up and be out of the door.'

Knock, knock and knock once more,
'Come on sleepy head, get out of your bed.'
'But, I just need more time,
My clothes then I'll find.
I'll be down for breakfast, just a little more time.'

'I'm sorry, I'm late,' my friend rushes by.
'I ran out of time, can't stop and chat.'
The rain and the wind heave a big sigh,
As I get to sit and talk with my cat.

'Why are people always in a rush?'
'They tell me that time waits for no one.'
So they queue, push and shove.

But isn't it true, time's on our side?
We do not know this, so from time we hide.
We take our time deciding whose time,
Will it be yours or will it be mine?

I don't know what time will bring,
But I do know a couple of things.
Time is our slave and not our boss,
There is time to prosper,
There's time to be lost.

Whatever the time and for whomever we call,
There is time for one and there is time for all.
Knowing which is whose time to be,
Knowing there's time, for you and for me.

Should I always listen to my friends and do what they say, or do friends sometimes get things wrong? Well, probably both are true at one time or another. We can learn to listen to our friends; this does not automatically mean that we always agree with them or that they are always right. Listening is quite a unique skill really, and one that is good to practise. I have found that listening to other people, rather than my talking all the time, gives my friends the opportunity to share with me what might be happening for them. If I talk all of the time, there isn't any space for them. This could convey to them that I am only interested in myself and I am not interested in them. If my friends believe this, then they would be unlikely to want to be my friends for very long.

All of us have our thinking coloured by our perceptions. So sometimes our friends will be wrong, because their perceptions won't be accurate. Perceptions are based upon our experiences, expectations and stereotypes. For example, we might have a concept about women drivers and reverse parking. This perception will colour our expectation of women drivers who reverse park their cars. Quite likely our expectation will be that these drivers don't do reverse parking very well! So, we then transfer this belief onto all women who drive cars. During a conversation a friend might say, 'Wow...you parked well! I didn't expect this.' If I were male, this friend would probably not have commented upon the accuracy of my reverse-parking ability, because it is often a given that males do this very well.

I know I went through a time when I took everything my friend said as 'Gospel'. That means I believed them all the time and accepted their words without question. After some time (many years) I began to question some of their rhetoric. I only did this though because of my own discomfort. I didn't know why I was uncomfortable or where it came from, nor what it meant or what I should do about it. I shared my discomfort with a different friend who, perhaps because they could be objective, was able to explain to me that my other friends had problems of their own and this coloured their interpretation of their life experiences. When I was with these friends, that perception spilled over into our relationship, and this was what was causing my discomfort. Once I knew what was happening, at least I could then tell myself, 'This discomfort is coming from my friends' perceptions. It isn't my discomfort and I don't have to wear it.' It's not very easy being uncomfortable, but it does help knowing why it's there!

Baring all has a code to it that is usually obvious to most people. I have found this to be problematic at times because I'm often the last person to know about the codes and unwritten rules that everyone else seems to know so well. There seem to be different rules for different areas. For example, within the social context of 'who's who and what's what' there is a keen desire by many to join in the gossip about others. I'm not into gossip and I don't see the value of it. But, what can I do when gossip is the sole sum of the conversation existing between my friends? If I don't join them, I am left out. If I do join them, I'm at a loss for what to say! Well, I tend to comment that I'm not into gossip, don't see the point of it and feel uncomfortable around it. At least my friends then know where I stand and I can give them the option to continue the conversation without me or change the tone of the conversation.

When it comes to 'baring all' in an academic way, I feel more comfortable. As long as the conversation is about something I am interested in, and I can share in it, then I am happy to be a part of it. It's a bit different if I'm not interested and don't have anything to contribute. But I have noticed that my friends might still need me to 'listen' to them even if I can't contribute to the debate. If I just up and leave because of my lack of interest, my friends might interpret this as a lack of interest in them. This can negatively impact upon our friendship as they may feel rejected by me. So I try to show interest, even when I am not interested. I feel uncomfortable about this, but that is a small price to pay for my friends' comfort.

Baring all politically? Politics is an area that can cause a lot of conflict between people, including between one's friends. I guess there are different areas in politics; some may be safer to discuss than others. When it comes to general politics, if there is such a thing, staying away from expressing strong opinions, especially if they are controversial, might be a good idea, but it's not something I have been good at! Of course, if one's opinions are invited (directly or indirectly due to circumstances) it's a different story, but if not, it might be best to refrain from expressing them in general conversation.

Having said this, I know that my personal views on some areas of social politics might be considered by some as extreme. I am very keen on the concepts of justice for all – including individuals of all races, religions, sexual preference (between consenting adults), political persuasion, family configurations, educational and employment status, able bodied or not and of various neurological diversification. At times I have been outspoken about this, and this has caused some grief to me and to my friends. No one seems to be against justice, but differing concepts of 'justice' seem to constitute differing belief systems for different individuals! For example, some don't believe in the concept of government support for individuals who, for a variety of reasons, are not able to work or are without employment. They would make a blanket statement that everyone should work and no one should be on 'benefits'; '...only this is "just" and proper,' they will say, because they believe it to be wrong that some individuals work for wages and others are given a 'free' handout. I have, on occasion, entered into debate with those of such a persuasion and have found it a pointless activity because they were not open to any other ideas on the matter. However, it might not be pointless if one were to enter such a debate with an open mind and an ear to listen to alternative views, experiences and ideas.

There are times when one's friends don't treat us as we would like or don't agree with us about something. This is common human behaviour. It does not mean though that we have to return the favour! Disagreement between friends is common and can usually be solved by our choosing to agree to disagree! I am learning that it is OK to have differing views from one's friends.

CHAPTER 8

It's Hard to
Be a Good Friend

'Friends will go anywhere with you. Friends take the good with the bad. Times that I have with my good friends are the best times that I ever had.' These words are of a song I remember from a while back. They have some specific memories for me after having sung it many times at a gathering of people (some were my friends) before a large convention. The meaning of these words took a while to sink in though. For example, it took me a long time to understand that the words were not meant literally. At times friends do not want to go somewhere with you, physically. The words metaphorically meant that friends would support you emotionally and be a friend to you even when they didn't agree with decisions you were making or things you were doing. So I guess it means friends might tell you that they disagreed with what you might be choosing to do, but were still your friends. Of course, even though our friends remain our friends, even when they don't agree with us, it doesn't mean they are always available to us. There are those times when you might need a friend but can't find a friend who's free for you. They, because of their own commitments, might not be available to you. Even though our friends would want to be able to support us and be there for us, they might not be able to. It's hard to be a good friend!

I have found myself in situations where I really needed a friend and I couldn't find anyone who could assist me. Either my timing was out (too late at night; friends were out; friends were occupied already) or those I chose to contact didn't feel that they were equipped to help me and I was passed on to someone else who also wasn't able to assist me! At such times in the past I have panicked, and this has made matters worse. These days I have a number of strategies that I can use either to prevent this situation from occurring in the first place, or to help diminish the difficulties if I'm in this kind of situation again.

Some ideas that might help in a time of need

First, preventative strategies

- If I know I might be in for a difficult time (emotionally or physically) I can arrange to have the phone numbers of a couple of friends who can be 'on call' throughout the day and/or night.

- If I know I have difficulties with a specific situation, individual or group, I can either choose not to be part of that situation, group or individual encounter, or I can aim to prepare for the situation so that I have some coping strategies available to me. For example, leaving early, joining in from a distance, stating what it is that I can cope with and any specifics I can't (loud, noisy atmospheres, bright lights, strong fragrances, etc.).

- I try not to take on more than I can cope with. For example, there have been times when I've said 'Yes' to something that I should really have said 'No' to. So, now I take a bit longer to process the circumstances around the event and then I can give a more realistic reply to any query or question. For example, 'Wendy, we are going out to dinner tonight, will you join us?' 'Yes, I can join you,' I

might reply. But actually when I have time to process this,
I realise that I haven't thought this through well enough.
First, I need to ask myself some questions about this before
I can know if I am *able* to join them for dinner; such as 'Do
I have the time tonight for this or should I be doing
something else? Where is this dinner happening? Will it be
quiet or will it be a loud, busy place? If it's loud and busy I
won't be able to sit there. How many other people are
going to this dinner?' In the past, on a few occasions, I
remember being invited to dinner expecting to be the only
guest, only to find there were others there too. I found this
distressing because it wasn't what I expected. I have gotten
to a place, seen my friends and then I've realised I can't
cope and have left. This isn't an easy or comfortable
situation for anyone, so it's better to 'weigh' things up first
and reply appropriately, rather than have to experience
such discomfort and regret.

- I sometimes recognise times when I know I am going to
  need a friend to support me. For such times, I find it useful
  to canvass my friends to see if one of them will be available
  to assist me. If I attempt to tackle a situation on my own,
  find that I can't cope and expect to get support
  immediately, I might find that no one is available at that
  time. It's better to check out availability first.

- Learning to be one's own best friend is an asset that has
  taken me a long time to value. Being kind to oneself and
  taking care of oneself are also ways of preventing some of
  the difficulties we might find ourselves in. By this I mean
  recognising our limitations and learning to abide by them.
  Of course, there are times when we stretch ourselves
  beyond our limitations, but only after adding up all the
  available information to check that we will be able to cope.
  Being kind to oneself also means not putting ourself into
  situations where we are certain to get into difficulties. This
  might not be understood by some people who are not on

the autistic spectrum, but we need to take care of ourselves, even though others might not understand or agree with us.

Second, strategies to assist when on the edge of a meltdown and a 'known friend' is not available:

For those of us with autism there might be times we have an *autistic meltdown*. This is when we find ourselves in a situation that is totally overwhelming and we can't cope. Some of us may rock ourselves, hum, pace up and down, cry with our hands over our ears and become irrational and out of control. These events are very scary for us and for other people around us. Although prevention is better than cure, in this situation it's too late for that!

- I guess the first thing is learning to recognise that we're not coping and need a way out of a potential difficulty. If we are alone (not with a friend) we may need to rely upon ourselves and any behavioural routines we might have practised for such occasions. I have learnt to say 'I'm going somewhere quiet now' or 'I need some quiet space' or 'I'll be back later to deal with this' or 'I was glad I came but I have to leave now', etc. Knowing myself well enough means that I can tell when I am beginning *not* to cope and I need to be out of the situation fast. If I miss this moment though, it may be too late to prevent overload and subsequent meltdown.

- It might be useful to carry an ID card that states 'I am autistic and I need to be taken to a quiet space to have some time to calm down'. Quite often local ASD support groups have such cards already made up. Otherwise we can make our own and put our own words on them. I have put some examples into the back of this book, along with some other ideas for cards that might be useful (Appendix 3).

- My calming down strategies include sitting down, and breathing in and out deeply, but slowly. I also like to feel soft material (the smooth leather of my wallet) and hum to myself.

- I might have the phone number on my card too so I can ask someone to phone home, if I can't do this myself, and ask a family member to come and get me.

- Ultimately, learning to be my own best friend is a good idea and I am happy to know that I can usually draw upon my own devices to assist myself in a calamity.

Discovering potential new friends. Yesterday I was waiting at the airport for a later flight because fog had caused the scheduled flight to be cancelled. A kind-looking middle-aged gentleman approached me and asked me if I had a Nokia mobile phone charger he could borrow. I didn't, but my travel companion did, so she lent him hers. Although I didn't get to spend much time with this gentle man (we shook hands, exchanged names and spoke briefly about our travel plans), I felt that had we had enough time we might have become friends. Sometimes one meets people who one feels comfortable with; such individuals are potential 'new' friends.

Having space in our lives for the discovery of potential new friends is always a good idea. It might be that our established friends have times when they are not able to meet up with us. If we are developing new friendships, then we are also increasing opportunities for further future companionship. A friend once said to me, 'You shouldn't put all your eggs into one basket.' She was trying to say that if all of your resources are together in one place, and that place is unavailable or can't be found, then you lose access to those resources. So, if we spread our friendships around a little more and don't keep them all in the one space, then we are more likely to have them available to us at different times.

Being demanding. I have a tendency to be quite demanding upon my friendships. Apparently I am inclined to wear people out! This being the case, it's a good idea to spread myself around a little thinly; rather than too thickly, too often, with the same friends!! I have some very good friends around the globe. I don't get to see them very often, but we stay in touch via email, phone and the occasional card or letter.

Good Friends

Good friends are here to stay,
Good friends hear what we say.
Good friends don't pull away,
Good friends say, 'We're OK.'

I once had this friend (so I thought) whom I trusted and respected. I don't know what happened for them to change their mind about me, but they gave up on our friendship and stopped being my friend. I wrote letters to them and tried very hard to find out what it was that they believed I had done, so that I could put it right. Unfortunately though, they never responded to me again. It's very uncomfortable living with the knowledge that you have upset someone but you don't know what you did or why they are upset. It's uncomfortable because you know they are hurting but you can't fix it. Ideally, keeping a check on one's friendships and aiming to develop good communication might prevent this type of event from happening, but there are no guarantees.

Misunderstanding can happen to anyone. I think it occurs because each individual involved comes to a relationship with their own past experiences and expectations. During the course of the friendship these experiences and expectations colour the interaction between us. As well as promoting a positive influence from some of our experiences and expectations, there can be a negative impact upon the concepts we each have of the intentions of the other. For example, if we have grown up with suspicion and mistrust as everyday companions, we will most likely transfer these attitudes to our friendships; if we have grown up with understanding and acceptance as our everyday experience, we will impute these attitudes upon our friendships.

Recently I was staying in the home of some very good friends. Although I would consider these friends to be close friends, and we have shared many intimate conversations, we are from differing backgrounds. I tend to be a very open person and, if anything, I am a bit too trusting. My friends are very private people and are more conscientious about their belongings and the security of their things. In some ways I am a bit of a slob, especially when it comes to clothes and presentation of self. I'm not too bothered about presentation, as long as it's clean and comfy. My friends, however, would go that extra mile and be inclined towards being a bit more upmarket, fashionable and presentable. Presentation, to them, is very important. So I am aware that there are times when we clash. A recent 'clash' occurred without my even noticing it! I felt a measure of discomfort, but could not work out why or where it came from. It was only as I talked over the events of our evening together, with another friend, that I was able to account for my feelings about what had happened – my expectations had not been met and I was feeling disappointment and rejection. The reality, however, was not that my friends were rejecting of me but that they related to me within the limits of their own comfort zones. I found this understanding helpful in facilitating my dealings with my feelings and I was able to let go of my hurt rather than allowing it to separate me from my friends.

'Variety is the spice of life,' a friend says, as they encourage me to do something in a different way. I think I can understand that for them always doing something the same way feels boring and they prefer a change. I have friends who don't enjoy watching the same movie twice, going on holiday to the same place more than once, eating in the same restaurant all of the time or wearing the same outfits of clothing. However, many of us as Aspies and Auties are quite the opposite. We may like to watch the same movies frequently, take holidays in the same place and at the same time each year, eat in the same restaurants all the time and wear particular sets of clothing all of the time. This can be difficult for our friends to understand because we are not like them. Maybe there is something comforting about being a certain way, and it's hard to imagine that others might be different to one's own way of being? But, actually, either way is OK. We might need our friends to accept that this is what suits us, and we might need to accept that they prefer it differently. Accommodating our differences might take a bit of work, but it can be done.

For example, I like to eat the same foods and don't like to try new food. Some of my friends find trying new foods an exciting thing to do and encourage me to try new foods too. I might attempt to do this with some types of foods, if they are familiar, but rarely will I try food I know I don't like. So, I enjoy bananas and cream, but I hadn't ever tasted banana cream pie. One of my friends said that it was like bananas and cream; I tasted it, they were right – I liked it. On another occasion, a different friend encouraged me to try some broad beans. I like baked beans, so they thought I would eat broad beans too, but I didn't like these beans at all! Then there are times when I won't try the food because it contains foods I know I don't cope with. Either the food has a texture I don't cope with, or a flavour or a fragrance. I accept that this is who I am. My friends try to accept this too; but they still challenge this in me at times, and that's OK. Good friends may have different likes about different things, such as food, clothing and political beliefs, but we can still all learn to accommodate who we are and enjoy sharing in the world that is 'friendship'.

It's Not Easy Being 'A Friend'

Saying what we mean to say,
Meaning what we say?
These two things are not the same,
They change from day to day.

If I am to trust in you,
And you to trust in me.
Then meaning in the words I use,
Must be the same for say and do.

If I say but do not do,
My words just will not ring out true.
If I do but do not say,
You might conclude you've grounds to sue!

What if the very words we speak,
Say different things for you and me?
I understood you to say 'Yes',
You were thinking 'Maybe yes'.

Your maybe, might do, probably and so,
Could be heard as definite and lead on into hope.
Hope that is shattered leads us to despair,
Why trust our friends anyway,
They obviously just don't care!

CHAPTER 9

Letting Your Friends
Know You Care

The Friendship Song

Some say that Summer will warm a fragile heart.
Others talk of music, or of walking in the park.
But Winter isn't always the reason for the cold,
It may be icy outside, Spring or Summer bold.
The hurting soul feels nothing, except the pain
    untold.

Chorus
When words are shared with another,
A secret world unfolds.
The joy of true acceptance
Brings you inside, out from the cold.

You took my hand and travelled too.
Through wind and rain, we sailed, us two.
My hurting heart, so torn apart,
Was wooed to life by you.

Chorus

My heart is stronger now, and warm,
As we continue upon Life's way,
We wake to face another day.
For, together we will brave the storm.

Chorus

Truer friends the world knows not,
Than you, my friends to me.
So while the seasons come and go,
The Summer rains or Winter snow.
I wish you only love to know.
For life will pass, but as we go,
Hear the pain of each other's soul.

Chorus

How easy it is to be smooched by a pet pussycat. They just rub themselves up against you and purr away. There is no doubt about their telling you that they are pleased to see you. But, how do we let our friends know that we are pleased to see them? How can we tell if they are pleased to see us? Rubbing up against them might not do it!

There are some traditional forms of greeting that cross many cultures and countries; hand shaking, for example, is one way of letting our friends know we are pleased to see them. But what about hugs and kisses? Most people don't think twice about giving a friend a hug. I have friends who are very uncomfortable with being hugged, even by close friends. They accept it from family and partner, often because they have to, but friends are not considered to fit that category. Usually, friends are seen, by some of us, as different to family, not the same, so different rules apply. For others of us, friends are with us to perform the role of travel companion, shopping guide, cinema mate, bowling pal, and so on. We might not even consider giving them a hug because it doesn't fit with the activity we share. Separating person from object of activity and seeing them as an individual does take a bit of working out. Some of us might need support with this.

If I were to ask each of you reading this book about your future hopes and expectations you might each give me a different answer. The one theme running through your answers, though, might be the need to know that your life, and those of the individuals you love, are going to be OK.

You might not be perfectly 'happy' all of the time, but you would like to have happy times and memories. You might not be perfectly healthy all of the time, but you would like to enjoy good health. You might not experience harmony in your relationships all of the time, but you would like to live at peace. Financially, yes you would like to be secure. When it comes to your family, you want the best for them...a good education, a career that pays well, marriage, grandchildren, and so on.

All of the above applies to our friendships too. If we don't talk to each other about these things, though, how will we know what we are each thinking? Letting our friends know that we love them will mean that we tell them so. But, how do we tell them?

I'm Listening, My Friend

The sunset is where day will end,
The oceans come and go.
As time leaves her mark on us,
In wisdom we will grow.

The sunset is where all begins,
As we each watch and ponder.
The sunrise follows and blackbird sings,
To greet each morn with wonder.

Wonder at the newest dawn,
As each new thing in joy is born.
Wonder at the life we're given,
As Angels sing their song in Heaven.

Today we echo loud and clear,
With rain and wind and sunshine.
Listen well and you might hear,
The hearts of friends we hold so dear.

Letting our friends know we care for them will also mean accepting them for who they are. I was having this discussion with my friend Katy Harris in Singapore. We discussed the issue of difference amongst our friends. The fact that each individual was different from another and that this meant they brought different attributes into the friendship. Not every friendship is deep and meaningful, just like not every friendship is fun-loving and jolly. Some friendships are seriously complicated, others are light-hearted, and some are happy to skirt around the edges of anything that seems good or useful at the time. But they will all bring with them treasures of one kind or another, and appreciating this isn't always easy to understand or to communicate.

For my friends who find the idea of touch too threatening, I like to send them an email or a card, just so they know I am thinking of them. I also have friends who would feel very uncomfortable writing words that would be read by others, and even words that I use to them privately would be too 'exposing' for them. So, even words are not always the right tool to use for everyone. If we have friends that feel this way, then finding a medium to convey our care for them will need careful thought. Maybe they would like us to send them flowers or go out with them to a place of interest for them? Maybe they would like us to leave them a small gift, like a book or CD? Maybe they need our help with some chores or household tasks? Whatever it is, we need to discover what pleases and conveys 'care' to our friends, without overdoing it.

Transition. Some of our friends come in and out of our lives and we may lose contact with them. These transitionary friendships are still important to us. I used to think that a friend should always be there when I needed them, but now I know that some friendships are meant to be transitory. A friend for a season, if you like. For example, we might have a friend at Summer Camp but not relate to them at other times.

Reading the signs. Perhaps many typical individuals are prompted by a number of things that help them think of their friends. I tend to think of my friends when prompted by appointments, or sometimes by birthdays, Christmas, and so on. So, for many of us, it's a bit like the Hansel and Gretel story where the characters are walking thorough a forest. During their walk they dropped breadcrumbs thinking they could use these to retrace their steps and find their way back. What happened? The birds came and ate the breadcrumbs; their means for retracing their steps were taken away. When it comes to friendships, this is the kind of thing that might happen to those of us less typical individuals. The usual signs and systems that people might use to detect their way in a relationship might not be obvious to us or might be gobbled up by other things that capture our attention.

Forgive the analogy, but often people are like flies with sticky legs. They buzz around life collating information. This seems to stick to them and they have little difficulty accessing it. They can offload their knowledge, sort it, put it all together arranged and know what they feel, what they need, what they would like, and more importantly, they know how to use that information appropriately.

It would be great if it were understood that we, as individuals with AS, are all different and probably even more different than most typical individuals. When my attention is all in one place, I'm connected to what I'm interested in and may, therefore, miss what I'm not interested in. This is because my interest has all of my attention. If I'm attending to and focused upon watching a video or whatever, how will I know that you are speaking to me? That my bladder is full? That I'm hungry, and so on…

Helping each other to 'connect' to what we each are saying or wanting from one another is essential. One good friend of mine tells a story about a lad who was very good at doing as he had been told. 'Stand still whilst I speak to you,' said a teacher (my friend explained that the teacher was actually telling the boy off). So, although he stood still, he then branched out into his own favourite topic because no one had actually explained to him about 'listening' and knowing what to do with what he had heard.

What are we interested in? What are my interests? Can we share an interest? Will this influence how we care for one another? I am the most motivated when I am interested. How many of us are really good at doing things we are not interested in? I may need boundaries set for my interest (Beatrice encourages me to have only four hours at the computer, not eight. During the four hours she prompts me to go for a walk every hour). This means I have one longish walk and several times of going up and down the stairs. If a walk isn't structured into my day, it won't happen. Caring for me might mean I need prompts and encouragement to do things that others find easy to do without prompting.

What are our goals? *Short-term goals*: getting up in the morning. What motivates you into getting up in the morning? Are you looking forward to another pleasant day? I anticipate chaos! I need to know what I can expect from each day. I need to make 'to do lists'. I tick off the events when they are done. Sometimes I need support to structure my lists, I always need support in structuring my day. I even need my 'free' time structured. As friends we can help one another by avoiding surprises and keeping to appointments.

Mid-term goals: we all have dreams. They might be different for each of us, and some might be more realistic than others, but they are real and need to be respected. I remember when I wanted to be a missionary (I was nine). Then I wanted to be a nurse. I tried very hard to make this dream come true. Unfortunately, although I did well academically, I failed miserably in the practical domains of this profession. For years I lived with a sense of failure and didn't want to attempt any new thing ever again. Then a friend explained to me that a car stationary in a car park could go nowhere. It had to have the engine on and be in gear to move forward. She said that life could be likened to a car. If we want our lives to go places, be fulfilling and have meaning, then we need to get up some courage and put our car into gear. So, even at the risk of failure, I chose to take a chance at life and at friendship. It's because of my dreams and the encouragement of my friends that I now set goals and explore ways of making them happen!

Learning how to know stuff is so invaluable. I especially need to know what I am feeling, what I should do with what I feel, where and when and how to recognise that I need support in this and who to ask for support. Is it OK to ask the bus driver? How can I know that you have feelings? How can I know what these are? I need you to share with me about what you feel. If you don't, I might conclude that you don't have any specific feelings about stuff, or I might believe that you will always feel the same as I do. I once heard my friend Rita Jordan say that trying to identify 'emotion' from a smiley face or a sad face cartoon picture isn't really how it is in real life.

Long-term goals: knowing how to relate to others is a constant goal for many of us. This is a great goal and needs lots of revisiting. We all need to be able to use the support that we share together as friends. I know that we all like to be independent and this is seen as a great goal too. But, in some ways, being independent isn't a goal for me; I have lots of that already. What I really need to learn is how to be interdependent!

Between us, our friendships can help to keep us sane. Most of us value the support of our friends. I know that I am good at a number of things. I love being out the front of a large group and performing on stage. The reality is that we all have areas of our lives we feel content with and in control of. Friendships, however, are enigmas that are constantly changing and constantly needing input from us. We should never think we know it all because this will mean we certainly don't.

I'm not good as a member of a group. There are too many things coming at me at once. I will probably never be comfortable in a big group. So, I choose to sit on the edge near an exit, come and go as I can, limit interaction, and so on. I'm caring for myself by doing this. My friends can support me by allowing me to do this. Maybe this is true for you too. Maybe we need to tell more people about what works for us so that they can understand Aspie friendships too.

Friends Along the Way
by Glenys Jones, my friend and fellow traveller

My very first friends were my brother and sister,
Very close in age, we played together and fought.
The friends they had, I shared as well,
Play indoors moved to play in the street.
Making dens, riding bikes, inventing games and
    covering our tracks when things went wrong or
    got out of hand,
We'd band together and survive the day.

Going to school was the next big jump,
Sitting next to a boy I'd never met,
Such was the emotion, his name is still with me –
    Malcolm.
Boys and girls together on tarmac – equal and
    daring,
Showing and telling, and sometimes in fights.

Then I moved to a school where my mother was
     teacher,
So plenty of friends came forward to play.
We played marbles and swaps in the playground at
     break
And sometimes formed gangs and lined up, face to
     face.
There then came selection – so many friends gone
I had to find new ones – had a strong sense of loss
My best friend became the girl who lived closest,
But still even then, we were four miles apart.
We shared homework by phone and stories in bed
When I stayed at her house overnight (now called
     sleepovers).

School friends remain strongly in mind,
I'm still in touch with a memorable few.
Some stayed in the area, others moved on
I no longer live there, but visit my mum.
So memories are kept alive by sights and sounds still
     there
Bus stops, the promenade, the schools, our old haunts
Take me back to where I was and with whom and
     why.

Looking back in time and thinking about friends,
They exist at many stages and different levels too.
Some I've known for many years and the shared
     experience is rich.
We're often very different, but connected by our past.
When I think of friendship now and how I would
     define it
The words of sharing; trusting; warmth;
     laughing; sadness; giving; taking;
     learning; and relaxing are those that spring to
     mind

Having common interests but other dimensions too
　　and liking to be outdoors and active
Have friend appeal to me.

On a final note, with a good friend,
Most things are synchronous,
Not much needing to be said,
Silence, decisions, annoyances disclosed.
All OK.
All accepted, as the essential core is love.

You might not think the following picture is very alluring, but Sweet Pea, a 'wild' cat who was fostered to live in the barn and keep the mice population controlled (the odd rat too I reckon), lived without human touch for two years. She did her job well, but when her pussy companion was killed, she seemed to so want to be close to her human owner, though her fears prevented her. Very, very gradually, over a long time, she succumbed to kindness. Today, although still wary, she loves having her head rubbed and has the loudest purr! She is a 'friend' of the family now, welcoming you as you approach the front door and wrapping herself liberally around your legs at dinner time.

Sweet Pea (a new friend)

Establishing friendship can take time and lots of reassurance. Sharing who we are and letting others see us in all our guises requires confidence. We each need that confidence echoed back to us telling us that we are each OK.

Friendship (by Elaine Hack, my friend whose trust I value)

For me now, at the age of 53, friendship means being comfortable with (that person). Doing things together; telling ourselves stories from our shared pasts; reminiscing – often without being able to remember the names, dates or places – do you remember? – oh you know – she used to be with – oh you know – we used to see her at – oh you know.

New friends – have to pass the comfortableness test – tall order – can it be done? Yes. Wendy is a new friend who behaves like an old friend – isn't in your face, wanting to be entertained all the time, doesn't intrude, looks after herself, interacts when she wants to, does her own thing (i.e. she is respectful, whilst also being very warm, funny and good company).

I think friendship meant something very different to me in my twenties; something very much more intense, no better or worse than what friendship means to me now, just very different.

One thing that is the same is that I like to be *doing* things with friends, not just sitting around chatting, particularly during daylight hours. I do enjoy intense discussion though about things that interest me.

Good friends:

- give each other time when they're needed
- take pleasure in each other's company or discourse
- consider each other's feelings
- are moved by each other's joys and pains, and rejoice or mourn together

- are supportive of each other's hopes and comforting of each other's fears
- do not cause each other avoidable pain
- make efforts to help each other
- have feelings which last – friendship feelings are mellow and enduring not volatile or feverish.

Dinah Murray (left; person-centred consultant), a friend who has seen me in some of my worst Autie moments, helped me through them, and loves me, just the way I am

In a friendless world a human being would be a poor vulnerable creature. Friends are like a safety net, so when we get knocked back we don't fall too far. Friendship is necessarily mutual, we are all part of each other's safety nets.

For each of us, letting our friends know we love and care for them might be a task that we facilitate differently, according to who they are, who we are, what the circumstances are and what we are each used to. We just need to check in regularly and not allow familiarity to breed contempt. Friendship is very precious, but should never be taken for granted.

CHAPTER 10

Sustaining and Developing Our Friendships

As we have seen by our reading in the previous chapters, caring for and developing our friendships can take time and commitment. It can be fun having a friend. It can be an adventure getting to know our friends better. We can go out together (cinema, bowling, art gallery, animal park) and that can be really good. On the other hand (seeing the other side), it can be a serious business too. Suddenly there are these expectations upon us, i.e. we have to think of others and their needs as well as our own. There are all sorts of ways to do this. Some of us may not find it very easy to work out what someone else's needs are, so learning to spot some of the signs can be helpful. For example, it seems that needs present according to category. There are:

- environmental needs
- sociability needs
- nutritional needs
- physical needs
- emotional needs.

The above are not written according to priority, but rather as they came to mind. Our order of need may change according to circumstances, which means we need to be alert to this. For example, on some occasions my physical needs (needs for sleep, shelter, warmth, comfort, etc.) may be stronger than my nutritional needs. So, although I may have food available to me, standing in the rain and cold might mean I am too uncomfortable to eat and I need to find shelter and warmth before I am comfortable enough to enjoy my food. I have experienced numerous occasions when in the company of friends I have misjudged their needs. My own need has been to talk, but their need was to focus upon something else (the television programme they were watching, for example), so in not noticing their needs but being taken up with my own I was causing them discomfort. To help me to accommodate my friends' needs I aim to note the circumstances they are in. If we can get this right we are halfway there in addressing the needs of our friends. So we can ask ourselves some questions, such as:

- Is this the right time for talking, or are my friends occupied by other things (TV, radio, other people, business, work, eating, being on the telephone, being in pain, being in bed, etc.), such that it would cause them inconvenience or discomfort to talk at that time?

- If my friends have just arrived to visit me, do they need refreshment?

- We have been entertaining some friends. Do they need to leave now?

- Is this the right conversation to have with our friends at this time? Maybe they are tired and listening to conversation will be uncomfortable for them?

- Does my friend need a hug? Why not ask them? Usually a hug to greet friends and to say goodbye when they leave is a good thing. But, hugs are intimate responses of affection and are not always welcome.

- Does my friend need cheering up? Maybe I could offer to help them in some way? Maybe sending them a card or a letter would be a useful thing to do?

- Maybe our friends are going through a tough time just now and just want our company or support but don't want advice?

If we have gone through our mental list (without actually speaking these questions in the form of a list) then we might be more likely to accommodate our friends. This helps to maintain our friendships.

To say or not to say, that is the question. Now there are times when our friends NEED to hear certain things from us. This can be a delicate issue. Have you ever been given a gift from a friend that you didn't like? Inside of yourself you will feel disappointment. You might even think 'if they really knew me they would know I wouldn't like this'. But in order to care for our friendships (and our friends) they need us to respond with appreciation, not anger or disappointment. Learning to feel one way but respond another way can be difficult. The rule is: I am allowed to be disappointed and feel uncomfortable, but I say 'thank you' and smile. My friend needs me to acknowledge that they have thought about me and have tried to show that. It is this that I am acknowledging, even if I'm not happy with their gift. This is why we have the saying 'It's the thought that counts'.

Sometimes we may know our friends so well and be so comfortable together that we can add (after our thank you and smile) words that let the person know we love and appreciate them but not their gift. Sharing our feelings without hurting their feelings requires our being tactful. If they ask us whether we like their gift, we can be honest. Perhaps we can explore ways together how to exchange it for something we really like better.

There are times when a friend just needs us to listen to them. They don't seek our advice so much as wanting us to be a sounding board that they can bounce thoughts and ideas off. If this is the case, and again we can ask them about this, then we need to try to accommodate our friends' needs and resist giving them advice or trying to suggest a way out of their issues.

A friend of mine was in tears when she had to leave her family in one country and return to her home in another country. Instead of one of her family members giving her a hug and wishing her a safe trip, they commented, 'Why are you crying? You chose to live abroad. You didn't have to.' These words wounded my friend and she felt sad. Sometimes, even though the words we state are accurate in their description, they are misplaced in their context. Getting context right is an art!

How can I remember their birthdays? Well, unfortunately, we might not always succeed. I aim to put important things to remember (birthdays, anniversaries, engagements) into my electronic organiser. I also write them on the current calendar and I use a reminder service that comes through my email inbox. So I do try hard to find ways to help me remember, but I still sometimes forget. My friends appreciate that I'm not good at being organised and they forgive me!

Should I buy them Christmas presents? You might like to buy Christmas presents for close friends. If I do this, I try to set an amount to spend which is reasonable and achievable for me. Of course, this may vary for each of us, but it is important to spend wisely and not be too extravagant or too miserly. Sometimes friends can make an agreement between themselves about what they will spend on one another for gifts at Christmas. This way we each know the range of what to spend, and it saves the potential embarrassment of any huge discrepancy between one another's cost of our gifts.

If I do want to buy them a gift for some special occasion, how can I find out what they would like? This can be a bit tricky. There are times when it seems fine to ask outright what someone might like. I have a friend who doesn't like surprises, so it's important for her to know what she is getting. We tend to go out together to the shop and she chooses her gift. The only thing that I suggest is the price range.

What if they buy me a gift and I don't like it? How can I be honest without hurting their feelings? I have commented on this scenario previously, but because it's so important I'll echo it again. I have noticed that in general when an individual receives a gift from a friend or family member that they respond with a smile and words to the effect of 'That's lovely. Thank you.' It seems that most people, even if they feel disappointed with the gift, can appreciate the thought behind it. So, when they say 'That's lovely. Thank you', they are caring for their friendship by allowing their friends to feel appreciated. If they reject the gift, quite often the friend feels rejected too. However, what can we do with our disappointment? Wouldn't our friends want us to be honest? Well, some might and they might even say, 'Look, if you don't like it we can change it.' But others won't understand and will think of our 'honesty' as bad manners.

The rule I follow is this: If our feedback is requested, we can politely say how much we appreciate them and their thinking of us, but when we don't like the gift we can ask if it's possible to change it. We can echo how much we appreciate them: 'Maybe we could go to the store together and exchange it?' If feedback is not requested or it's not possible to comment on how I feel about the gift, then I accept it with dignity and am very thankful. We are allowed to feel disappointment, but we must show our appreciation for the giver.

Caring for our friendships takes time and effort. Just like we want our friends to give us some of their time, we need to do the same for them. Some friends can be 'high maintenance', and we might need to see them little and often. Other friends are much easier to be with and take very little from us. Friends come in all shapes and sizes, but usually friendship is a two-way encounter and should be a unique and special relationship for each of us.

Friends on friendship

Some of my friends who have written about friendship below have been my friends for more than 20 years. Others I have only known for less than five. Their ideas, opinions, impressions and experiences of friendship are real, personal, revealing and ongoing. These friends are all in friendships with me after I moved from England to Australia, but they don't all reside in Australia. Friendship is a global phenomenon, and it carries us through the years and stays with us wherever we live in this constantly changing world. Friendship is the one thing I count upon to be steady and reliable. Friends may not always meet these criteria, just as I might not, but friendship per se does.

Judy Mason

Friendship is mysterious to me. What makes one person a friend and another someone who you like but don't necessarily want to spend time with? Why do you click with one person almost immediately and get to know them better over time, while you take longer to decide that you really like another? I'm still amazed when I remember how I met one of my oldest friends. On our first day of high school I was wandering around feeling somewhat lost because I didn't have any particular friends. I noticed another girl who looked as lost and alone as I felt, so I went over to her and said, 'Let's be friends.' I was 14; she was 12. Today, more than 40 years later, we're still friends, in spite of losing touch with each other for about 30 years and only getting back into contact about

Judy Mason (left). One of my oldest friends who has travelled with me through doubt, fear, uncertainty and disappointment; and stayed. She is a librarian and student writer in Perth, Western Australia

ten years ago. We became friends first and got to know each other later.

Wendy is another friend who I liked and was drawn to on our first meeting, although I didn't know much about her when we first met. Over time, she also has proved to have all of the qualities I look for in a good friend.

Some of the qualities I value in a friend are honesty, loyalty, intelligence, an open mind, a sense of humour similar to mine, integrity, depth of character and a sense of fun. Some of those qualities are apparent when you first meet someone, but some only become apparent as you spend more time with a person and get to know them. My high school friend has proved to have all of these qualities, but I didn't know that would prove to be the case on the day we met.

To me, a friend is someone who knows you well and accepts you for who you are. You can be honest with each other because you trust each other. You might not agree on all subjects, but that doesn't matter as long as you respect each other's right to differ. On the other hand, for me it's important that a friend shares most of my basic values, because if they don't, it's hard for me to respect them. For example, I could not be friends with someone who didn't value and practise honesty.

Because I'm introverted, I like to have only a few close friends, and I don't need to see them very often for us to remain close. There are people I see quite regularly and can spend time chatting with comfortably, but I consider them to be acquaintances rather than friends because we only talk about fairly superficial things. There are other people, such as Wendy and my high school friend, who I only see once or twice a year or even less, but when we're together we talk freely and openly about deep and personal matters. These are the people I consider to be my true friends.

Don Cameron

Writing about friends reminds me of a scene from the movie *Fried Green Tomatoes*. The lead actress says to her friend, 'You know what I think the most important thing in life is. Friends.' This was a statement from a woman who had lived a long and full life. So I agree very much with that. It takes a lifetime of experience to decide what really matters.

After much thought about friendship issues I decided that to make a list might help. Friendship is about: support, love, commitment, honesty, being a friend to yourself, patience, trust, creativity, hardship, risk taking, simplicity, courage, sometimes expecting something in return, sometimes expecting nothing in return, stepping back and trying to see another point of view, humour, being positive, being angry, experiencing time apart, surrender, acceptance of differences and an acceptance that the friendship does not have to endure, no matter what.

Does everyone need a friend? Most do. Is it important to be on good terms with yourself first? Yes. Being on good terms with everyone is probably the most difficult thing that people face.

Don Cameron, a horticulturalist, has been a quiet, consistent friend of mine for many years. One of 'The Boys' whom I can count on and trust

Myself, I have a small group of friends that are lifelong. Sometimes I don't see some of them for long periods, for months or even years. That's OK because the relationship endures and it's reassuring to know that the person is just a phone call or email away. Help would be there if needed.

Family of course are friends as well, but there is often an obligation to maintain that relationship.

My relationship with one friend exposes me to some levels of intimacy that I am not used to. This friend expects a greater level of intimacy than I am accustomed to. This I still find challenging.

To achieve a balance between the degree of intimacy that's right, for both, can be tricky.

Both children and the older generation in general seem more relaxed to enjoy being and having friends. Pressures, expectations, insecurities, social differences, etc. are not an issue.

There is much more that could be said about something that is so simple, yet something that does require effort.

Allan Schmidt

Friends awaken the very me inside of me. Strangers are potentially dangerous and have behaviours that infuriate. Friends are welcoming and warm like the winter sun. They are a place of rest, a watering hole and a sidewalk café in a world that becomes more bureaucratic and political by the minute. Friends are gathered throughout a lifetime. They are family, my collective and tribe.

Allan Schmidt is a nurse, singer, songwriter and long-time friend to many, including me

We rejoice together, we weep together and support each other to stand when the very ground from under us seems to slip away. I stand naked before my friends all scars and warts. There is a knowing and secret mystery that binds us together.

I feel safe to expose the vulnerable sides of each and every face that I possess and expect nothing less back from my friends. They are a mirror as I try to grasp and wrestle with the meaning of everything that life throws and gives. We grow together; a beautiful garden, nurtured vines and flowers that tell a story within a story about us and all that time.

Friends give meaning to my life and become a measure to me to see where I've been. They reflect back to me those specific moments of when we met; significant crossways that linger and echo throughout our friendship. These make me who I am today.

I love my friends for who they are and what they mean to me. They are sacred, my church and map to understanding the supreme. I feel loved!

Glenys Reed

The friends I have are a very important part of my life. I treasure the times when we can be together, sharing many parts of each other's lives.

Glenys Reed (left) was once my next door neighbour and still my friend

I love to do different things with different friends, for example going for a walk, sharing a drink or a meal, playing golf or going on an outing to the movies, the footy, cricket or to a concert.

I don't have many friends, but those that I do have are very special people who listen to me and are always able to make me feel better if things aren't going too well. I hope I can return this feeling when things are not going well in their lives.

Making friends can be hard for people who find it difficult to meet new people. I never know if what I am saying is the right thing to say at that particular time. Sometimes the reactions of these new people make you want to hide under a rock, so when you finally make a friend they are extremely important.

To be a good friend you have to have the ability to listen to each other's problems and to react compassionately. Sometimes just listening will suffice, and having someone to talk to is vitally important. On other occasions you need to offer help and ideas, without being overbearing or pushy. It can be a difficult balancing act, but when you help your friend it is a very rewarding experience. I hope I am able to achieve this with my friends, even sometimes.

Friends enrich my life and I am thankful for their continued presence in my life.

Paul Martin

I am a raging extrovert! In other words, I thrive on the company of other people. I feel energised by company and relish good friendships. Due to my personality I tend to bare my soul to other people easily. I am also someone who tends to trust very easily. Most of the time this has helped a lot to develop good, long-lasting, deep relationships. Unfortunately there are some people who have abused this trust and my kind-heartedness. These experiences have left me shocked and hurt with a feeling like a light concussion. I recently experienced this where someone I had become very close to told me that they really wanted to cause me emotional pain, without any explanation or reason. When the hurt and anger gradually faded, I realised there are some people out there who are very damaged, and I need to cut ties with them and not reconnect under any circumstances. I must not allow myself to be vulnerable and emotionally attached to people who

Paul Martin is a psychologist living in Brisbane. He is also one of my 'oldest' friends and one whose journey in life has often paralleled my own.

abuse me. I am grateful that I haven't become bitter as a result, I just try and learn from each experience and hold back a little more until I get to know someone.

In stark contrast to this, I have experienced a wonderful friendship with Wendy for more than 20 years! I remember when my parents talked about friendships they had that were 20 years old, I used to think – God, they sound so old when they say that. Well now it is my turn to sound old!

My relationship with Wendy is one of the few relationships I can guarantee will last until the day one of us dies. It started through a Christian group that we co-led. We seem to have many strange parallels over the years, even though we are such different people. We were struggling with the same issues and at the same time came to the conclusion that the group we were leading was not for us any more. I feared that she would reject me, and she was thinking the same. We didn't realise at the time that the endless cappuccinos at the pizza shop up the road, dramas with her husband, my co-parenting of her children, struggles we shared with sexuality, finances, the tears, laughter, champagne and hugs had all combined to create a very strong foundation that has only grown in time.

The time and effort we both put into getting to know each other in the early days also created a safety net that would be important when I was confused about some of Wendy's behaviours. Before any of us knew that Wendy was an Aspie, none of us really had a framework that gave us an explanation as to why she would react in such strange ways at times. Due to my commitment to her as a close friend who I trust 100 per cent and disclose everything to, I was determined not to allow these unusual moments to change my feelings towards her.

When Wendy felt rejected or was being emotionally abused by someone she felt particularly close to, she could react in ways that for me seemed very strange. I also used to wonder why she would become a different person at a party, going from my confident, smiling, loving person to being anxious, at times even trembling, and would temporarily lose all basic social skills. There were many other times when I used to look at Wendy's unusual behaviour and inside would remind myself that no matter what Wendy does, and no matter how strange it looks, this can never change how we feel about each other. At times it was difficult to defend Wendy when people asked questions about her, but people always knew that we were very close and I wouldn't allow negative criticism.

When I found out about Wendy being an Aspie, it was as though I had wiped the steam off the windscreen and the road was so clear! This was such a relief for me as it gave me something to tell other people about so they could in retrospect understand Wendy's behaviours. For me it meant a lot as I also had a deeper understanding of what her needs are and to make sure that she is not placed in situations where she feels uncomfortable. This has meant many compromises over the years and some effort. For me doing these things is never a chore, they are like little gifts to a friend I love very deeply.

Over the years we have seen each other go through a lot of pain, experiencing many difficult challenges, and through this we have seen each other grow. The little time we have together these days is spent in a frenzy of conversations and often disclosing things to each other that we would normally keep to ourselves. For me, my relationship with Wendy is a model of a solid, healthy, long-term friendship. We respect each other, show each other little acts of love and kindness, demonstrate honesty even when it feels uncomfortable, encourage each other, give advice when necessary and laugh together. In our smiles to each other over the years, we are reminding ourselves of the joy and fulfilment of our life-long connection.

Mary Anne Faye

Wendy and Beatrice are new friends of mine. It's great to make new friends, particularly as you get older because I notice that as I get older I make fewer friends; probably because I don't often

Mary Anne Faye and Morris Gleitzman, at home with Bad Cat (as fellow writers and new friends these guys are just the best)

leave my home, but also because Life is busy. Sometimes I fear I only have so much emotional space, and that I might have to delete an old friend if I take on a new one. But that isn't the case as it turns out. What I realise is that there are lots of ways of having friends. There are the sort you don't see much, but think about lots, there's the sort you don't think about much but are always pleased to see, there are the few you see heaps and think about heaps, the ones you talk on the phone to regularly, and ones you wouldn't dream of talking on the phone with, the ones you actively do things with, and the sort you sit and eat with. Possibly my favourite sort. Depending on what we're eating of course. And then of course there are email friends.

There are friends whose lives are always in upheaval, who are fun because they often have dramatic stories to tell, and friends who are calm and soothing.

I suppose just as you have different clothing for different weathers, there are different friends for different feelings and occasions.

When you first meet a potential friend you don't really know what category they will fall into, or even if they might start their own category, and that's one of the things I enjoy about new friends.

One of the things I love is when a new person comes into your life, it's like beginning a gripping new novel, one where you just want to find out what happens next. I always look forward to the next visit, to find out what has happened in their lives, what they are thinking, what issues have been resolved, what haven't, how they are similar to me, how they are different, and what their new plans might be. And it's great if they are also interested in what I am thinking and feeling. That makes it two-way, and that to me is friendship.

When I think of a friend, I usually can't help but smile.

Morris Gleitzman

One of the reasons, I think, why stories have stayed at the centre of our culture since we first started telling them to each other in caves is that stories help us understand what goes on inside other people. They help us understand what's going on inside ourselves as well, and just how similar we are, despite all the differences, to every other member of our species. Stories, I reckon, teach us how to be friends.

The other thing that has taught me how to be friends is friends. When a friend offers me trust, generosity and love, I don't have to suspend disbelief to accept it. Few stories engage me as much as the unfolding sagas of my friends' lives. Few things move me as much as their desire to be a part of my life.

Friends are the people who don't laugh when they see the pile of neatly folded jeans in my wardrobe, stacked with the darkest on the bottom, moving up through subtle gradations of blue to the lightest at the top. And if they do, I don't mind.

David Heyne

What a special topic – having and being friends – and what a privilege to be invited by you, Wen – my very dear friend – to include some reflections on this topic. To be honest, I think my current reflections might be different to those I might possibly make some years down the track, because having friends and being a friend are virtues which keep developing over the years. I learn a lot about being a friend by having friends, and vice versa.

Right now, what I find myself valuing most in my friendships is acceptance: an open ear, an open mind, an open heart. It's not necessary (or even good) for me that my friends share all of my philosophies on the small stuff and the big stuff in life. What matters most is that friends can respect my ideas and perspectives, sometimes being 'reflective sounding boards' when I need to air and explore my philosophies, and sometimes being 'corrective

*David Heyne (an Aussie psychologist living in Amsterdam) has
taught me the meaning of 'soul mate'. As with my friendship with
Paul, Dave's friendship to me is a foundation and springboard that
has enabled other friendships to blossom.*

sounding boards' when they perceive that it might be helpful for
me to reconsider some of my ideas and perspectives.

It sounds like quite a lot that I ask of friendship. Do I sometimes run the risk of expecting too much of my friends? Probably.
And sometimes expecting too much of my friends can get in the
way of just enjoying my friends. And yet these precious people
continue to be friends with me. That is indeed the stuff of friendship: being accepted and respected even when my expectations
might be unhelpfully high at times. Friends are patient and for-
giving souls, patient with me and with my foibles.

Acceptance and respect make for a lovely 'easiness' between
friends. I don't mean a nonchalant sort of easiness that consists of
always just agreeing with each other. But an easiness that comes
from knowing that I am understood and valued by my friend, and
an easiness which means that there can be a real pleasure in just

being together and doing things together. Having friends offers so much in terms of both growth and pleasure in life.

For me, being a friend for others means being mindful of what other people might value in friendship. What is important for them? What do they need at this time? Sometimes the answer can be as simple as thinking about the things I value in friendship, because the things that I value may be some of the same things that my friends also value: an open ear, an open mind, and an open heart. At other times, it will be other things that my friends value most.

It is no surprise, of course, that being a friend shapes who I am, encouraging me to think beyond myself; giving is inter-twined with receiving. We heard it as kids – it is better to give than to receive – and as an adult I now see this maxim in practice, in the giving and receiving of friendship. And sometimes it means giving in a friendship at a time when it feels like I receive less from the other, and sometimes it means receiving more from a friend than I am probably offering to them as a friend. I've often missed the boat, failing to see what my friends might most value at a par-ticular time. And sometimes I've underestimated how important my friendship is for someone else.

Together, friends hold the tension between giving more and receiving less, giving less and receiving more. 'Being a friend' and 'having friends' cannot really be regarded as separate things. They're so intertwined. Thankfully so! And thankfully there are special people in my life – including you, Wen – who have shaped and blessed me through the 'give and take' in our respective friendships.

Cohen Morrison

I enjoy friendship with my friends, my family and other people in my life.

I get confused looking at people's faces and don't know if they are evil or nice.

My friend and fellow artist Cohen Morrison

I have always loved Thomas the Tank Engine series since I was very small.

Thomas is always a good friend to have and I get lots of enjoyment and excitement from watching new episodes. You may think that I am addicted to Thomas and some kids' TV shows – well I am.

I have lots of friends in my daydreams and TV shows, and it will always be.

My dog Sam, who is a female Maltese is so lazy, silly, does not go walking with us and sometimes goes to the toilet inside our house, is my very special friend, and I love her. She talks to me with her mind.

I will always make new friends, maybe from all around the world would be good. I would like to have a famous celebrity as a friend, also to be friends with the very poor and all the children who are abused.

I do not talk much to people, I spend a lot of time with my daydreams and my dog. I like it like that.

The above comments on friendship from some of my friends are as individual as they are, and yet they echo so many sentiments that so many of us identify with. Maintaining one's friendships in good order, allowing for growth and development in our personal lives and friendships and looking after ourselves are all aspects of fuelling the right choices. I am excited about my friendships and about the potential for making a difference in the world through the medium of friendship. Whether we are part of a scheme that supports a child in some distant place or whether we are supporting a friend here at home, friendship is powerful medicine!

★ ★ ★

I set out an extract of a conversation with Liam in Chapter 5. Liam has been getting on with his life and some interesting things have been unfolding for him.

Liam: What I've been realising is that I can be friends with other people, but I won't be friends with them in the same way as others might be. I can't easily follow their conversation and I get fed up with smiling all the time. I feel like an idiot. All of my life I have blamed myself for not being able to keep up with understanding the words that people speak to each other. Well, I'm realising that I don't have to! It's OK to be me.

When I am with other people, I feel so worn out trying to keep up with everyone; it can be exhausting. It occurred to me, as I've been processing this over and over, that some people might be good with words but, unlike me, they might not be very practical. Sometimes I want to say something about this. I am beginning to see that I can accept that I am different and have some very good skills that others may lack. Yes, I'm beginning to 'see' who I am and accept 'me'.

I think, in the past, my monotropism has caused me to have tunnel vision and only see my failure. I've just wanted to die. In many situations around other people who are all chatting away and understanding of one another, I have coped by drinking alcohol and by avoiding people. This new understanding, also very monotropic because I just keep going over and over it, is helping me to see that I don't need to do that. I can be me, amongst others, and that is OK.

Wendy: This is a huge thing for you. What triggered this revelation do you think?

Liam: I think it's just our going over the same ground time and time again…and you sticking with me, as my friend. You haven't given up on me. You are showing me that I am acceptable, just the way I am.

Wendy: This is fantastic…we need to celebrate this reality by practising and reaffirming these concepts often. I value your friendship to me. We all need one another in differing ways because none of us can be all things to all people all of the time. You understand things that I find difficult and you help me to discover my abilities in areas I usually avoid. Other things you do so well are not my 'thing' at all, but they are yours, so we share this. I can give you ideas and opportunities, you can give me your take on them, we share together. This is a wonderful discovery of life! A beautiful episode in an ongoing saga, that we are privileged to be taking together. Thank you for letting me be your friend and for being my friend on a journey that is the biggest adventure I have ever taken.

This morning, when I awoke and thought again about the conversation with Liam, I was reminded how difficult a journey friendship can be, but also how rewarding. Friendship for each of us could be a road to discovering life in a new and precious way. I recommend this journey to you and am sending all good vibes for a very pleasant trip!

★ ★ ★

Below are some quotes from a Friendship Calendar and from www.friendship.com.au/quotes. I hope you enjoy exploring them and exploring the friendship journey.

Never explain yourself. Your friends don't need it and your enemies won't believe it. *Belgicia Howell*

A real friend is someone who walks in when the rest of the world walks out.

You can make more friends in two months by becoming really interested in other people, than you can in two years by trying to get other people interested in you. *Bernard Meltzer*

To the world you may be just one person, but to one person you may be the world.

Do not save your loving speeches for your friends till they are dead. Do not write them on their tombstones, rather speak them now instead. *Anna Cummins*

Friends are like good melons…to find a good one you must try one hundred. *Claude Mernet*

Where you go, I will go; and where you lodge I will lodge; Your people shall be my people and your God, my God. *Ruth 1:16*

Appendix 1

Personality Test Just for Fun

Created by Ulla Zang (1994–2005) and used with her kind permission.

The copyright of all images and text in Appendix 1 belongs to Ulla Zang. No images or text may be copied, reproduced, used to prepare derivative works of, distributed or publicly displayed without the permission of Ulla Zang.

Each of the coloured squares (see back cover) has a corresponding personality profile. Although this test is 'just for fun' it is important to consider one's personality profile in relationship to one's friends. Sometimes our personalities clash and, because of this, certain individuals make better friends for us than others.

Discover your personality profile. Which picture draws you the most? The following relates to the pictures from 1 to 9 in their order, 1, 2, 3 being the top line, and so on.

Square 1. Carefree, playful and cheerful. You love a free and spontaneous life. And you strive to enjoy every moment, in accordance with the motto 'You only live once'.

You are very curious and open about everything new. You thrive on change. Nothing is worse than when you feel tied down.

You experience your environment as being versatile and always good for a surprise.

Square 2. Independent, unconventional and unfettered. You demand a free and unattached life for yourself that allows you to determine your own course. You have an artistic bent in your work or leisure activities.

Your urge for freedom sometimes causes you to do exactly the opposite of what is expected of you.

Your lifestyle is highly individualistic. You would never follow trends.

On the contrary, you seek to live according to your own ideas and convictions, even if this means swimming against the tide.

Square 3. Introspective, sensitive and reflective. You come to grips more frequently and thoroughly with yourself and your environment than do most people.

You detest superficiality. You'd rather be alone than have to suffer through smalltalk.

Your relationships with your friends are very strong, which gives you the inner tranquillity and harmony that you require.

You do not mind being alone for extended periods of time. You are rarely bored.

Square 4. Harmonious, balanced and down-to-earth. You value a natural style and love that which is uncomplicated. People admire you because you have both feet planted firmly on the ground and they can depend on you.

You give those who are close to you security and space. You are perceived as being warm and human.

You reject everything that is garish and trite. You tend to be sceptical toward the whims of fashion trends. Your style is easy and elegant.

Square 5. Pragmatic, confident and professional. You take charge of your life, and place less faith in luck and more in your own deeds. You solve problems in a practical, uncomplicated manner.

You take a realistic view of the things in your daily life and tackle them without wavering.

You are given a great deal of responsibility at work, because people know that you can be depended upon.

Your pronounced strength of will projects your self-assurance to others. You are never fully satisfied until you have accomplished your goals.

Square 6. Peaceful, discreet and non-aggressive. You are easygoing and independent. You do not need to be the centre of attention, instead you graciously let others take centre stage.

You have no set plans, rather you prefer to 'go with the flow', relying on your sharp instincts and intuition as situations present themselves to you. You are very social and popular, yet you are perfectly happy going off alone to pursue your interests. There is a quiet confidence about you.

Square 7. Analytical, trustworthy and self-assured. You appreciate high quality and things that endure. Consequently, you like to surround yourself with little 'gems', which are often overlooked by others.

Culture and tradition are important to you.

You have found your own personal style, which is elegant and exclusive, free from the whims of fashion.

Your ideal, upon which you base your life, is sophisticated pleasure.

Square 8. Romantic, dreamy and emotional. You are a very sensitive person. You refuse to view things only from a sober, rational standpoint.

You listen to your feelings. It is important for you to have dreams in life.

You reject people who scorn romanticism and are guided only by rationality.

You refuse to let anything confine the rich variety of your moods and emotions.

Square 9. Dynamic, active and extroverted. You are quite willing to accept certain risks and to make a strong commitment in exchange for interesting and varied work.

Routine, in contrast, tends to have a paralysing effect on you.

What you like most is to be able to play an active role in events. In doing so, your initiative is highly pronounced.

Appendix 2

On-line Friendship
and Support Agencies

www.unoduo.com
I found this a very interesting site on all types of friendship (looking for friends, travel companions, sporting partners, etc.) that was easy to use, FREE and world wide!

www.friendfinder.com
Also a FREE site, but incorporating romantic friendship sites and a chat room.

www.seniorfriendfinder.com
Another FREE site, linked with the one above.

www.carersonline.org.uk
This site gives advice and support to carers of individuals with disabilities or the elderly. It also helps with locating respite and holidays.

www.assupportgrouponline.co.uk
Autism and Asperger's support online.

www.relate.org.uk
Relate, the UK's largest and most experienced relationship counselling organisation, helps people work through their relationship difficulties and reach their own decisions about the best way forward. Tel: 0845 130 4010.

Google is a great search engine for finding home pages and websites for autism and Asperger's related information, including friendship.

Appendix 3

Autism Alert Cards

Below are some ideas that could be adopted and adapted as Autism Alert Cards. You don't have to use the words printed in these cards though, you can use words that suit you and the reason for your card.

Putting in your own photograph and contact details, as well as contact details of someone you might like to have contacted on your behalf in an emergency situation or when it's too overwhelming to find words to deal with a situation yourself, can be useful. I have used PowerPoint to create the cards below.

Autism Alert Cards

> Person with Autism
> Emergency Alert
> PLEASE READ

Please NOTE

- My name is:
- Sometimes it is hard for me to speak. I've handed you this card because I am too anxious to talk just now. I need a few minutes and a safe place to calm down.
- If you need to contact someone on my behalf please call:
- Name:
- Number:

Please NOTE

- My name is:
- I am tactile defensive and find touch uncomfortable. Please do not touch me or I may react defensively.
- If you need to contact someone on my behalf please call:
- Name:
- Number:

Autism Alert Card

- Name
- Address
- Phone number

- I need your support
- I'm not able to talk just now. Please call the person named below:
- Name
- Number

Autism Alert Card

- Name
- Address
- Phone number

- I'm having a difficult time understanding at the moment.
- I just need some quiet time to process what is happening.
- I'll phone you soon.

To My Friend

- I value your friendship, but I need some time and a safe space to calm down just now.
- Please help me to get home.
- Then please leave me for a while.
- I will phone you soon.
- Thank you

Speech evades me just now, please read this card

- I have given you this card because I need some space to think.
- Please don't ask me questions at the moment.

Thank you

Your friendship is important to me, please read this card

- I tend to say 'Yes' to most things but I might not have thought this through.
- Please remind me of this and give me some time to get back to you on this matter.
- You are a good friend and I appreciate you.
- Thanks

Index